TOTTENHAM
HOTSPUR
A HISTORY IN FIFTY CLASSIC MATCHES

TOTTENHAM
HOTSPUR
A HISTORY IN FIFTY CLASSIC MATCHES

STEWART PETERS

TEMPUS

Frontispiece: Tony Parks enjoys his moment in the spotlight after winning the UEFA cup for Spurs.

Front cover: Paul Gascoigne celebrates his goal in the 1991 semi-final against Arsenal.

Back cover: Spurs players celebrate their 1967 FA Cup final win against Chelsea.

The back cover picture is reproduced with the kind permission of Roy Brazier and the late Alan Rosenthall.

First published 2005

Tempus Publishing Limited
The Mill, Brimscombe Port,
Stroud, Gloucestershire, GL5 2QG
www.tempus-publishing.com

© Stewart Peters, 2005

The right of Stewart Peters to be identified as the Author
of this work has been asserted in accordance with the
Copyrights, Designs and Patents Act 1988.

British Library Cataloguing in Publication Data.
A catalogue record for this book is available from the British Library.

ISBN 0 7524 3612 0

Typesetting and origination by Tempus Publishing Limited.
Printed in Great Britain.

Introduction

It has not always been easy being a Spurs supporter. Having first been introduced to the club as a young child during the Keith Burkinshaw era, I was brought up on the highly successful cup-winning sides of the early 1980s, where my heroes included Glenn Hoddle, Ossie Ardiles, Ricky Villa, Garth Crooks and Steve Archibald. I can still recall aspects of the first game I ever went to at White Hart Lane. I was only five years old; Garth Crooks was in his first season at the club having signed from Stoke City and was on fire. My Dad told me that Crooks was sure to score and when he did, I remember being shocked by the volume of the home crowd's cheering as everyone stood up to celebrate the goal. Of course, there were still standing areas in those days and the attendance was far bigger than the capacity at the ground today. For a young boy, those images stay with you and, although partially intimidating, instil in you a flavour that you want to taste more and more.

Of course, before I was even born, Spurs had enjoyed periods of success that will forever cement their place as one of the great clubs in English football. The great Bill Nicholson's double-winning side of 1961 has been suggested as the finest club side ever to grace the English game and, ten years prior to that, manager Arthur Rowe's 'push and run' side stormed all before them in racing to the club's first ever league championship. It all began a long time before that, however, under a lamppost in Tottenham High Road to be precise, where the origins of Tottenham Hotspur Football Club can be traced.

That great side of the early 1980s won two FA Cups and a UEFA Cup, and you tend to think that the glory will remain intact for as long as you support the club. Spurs had some success in the late 1980s and early 1990s, but their reputation as a whole has fallen a fair way since then. Like I say, it has not always been easy being a Tottenham fan. To watch a team that was hailed as one of the 'big five' of English football when I was growing up gradually becoming a mid-table side that carries the much-undesired title of 'sleeping giant' is not easy to take. It is difficult to pinpoint exactly when Spurs began falling behind those that are considered the best in today's game but, with a club that has the size and tradition of Tottenham Hotspur, there is always hope of reaching greatness, a goal that has perhaps become more attainable with the structure currently in place, where present manager Martin Jol appears to have the club heading in the right direction.

Spurs supporters get a lot of criticism from the press for being too cynical and fickle when things are going badly or for being unrealistic when it's going well, which is partially true but, in my view, they are the best supporters in England. Of course, fans of every other team in the land would say the same thing, but you only have to sit among the Spurs fans on their travels to realise that the passion for their club goes far beyond one particular game. It is a passion that stretches through a rich and decorated history, embedding itself in each and every supporter like a lifelong soul mate.

Ricky Villa slides the ball under Manchester City goalkeeper Joe Corrigan for the winning goal in the 1981 FA Cup final.

Spurs fans love to talk about history but, in the case of Tottenham Hotspur, it is well founded. Few clubs can boast such championed names as Bill Nicholson, Alf Ramsey, Danny Blanchflower, Dave Mackay, John White, Jimmy Greaves, Alan Mullery, Martin Chivers, Glenn Hoddle, Ossie Ardiles, Paul Gascoigne, Chris Waddle, Gary Lineker, Gary Mabbutt and Jurgen Klinsmann, while boasting a fine collection of major honours and proudly having one of the largest fan bases in Europe. Looking to the future too, the current Tottenham squad offers the real prospect of sustained success, with England internationals Paul Robinson, Ledley King, Michael Carrick and Jermain Defoe in the ranks, together with a vast number of promising youngsters. In charting this history of Tottenham Hotspur Football Club, I have tried to recount, through a series of fifty matches, all the major moments that have made this club what it is today. In doing so, I would like to thank a couple of people. Firstly, the appropriately named Wyart Lane of the Spurs fanzine *My Eyes Have Seen The Glory* for providing some of the information regarding team line-ups and match details, and secondly my father, Geoff, for not only letting me sift through one of the largest personal collections of match programmes ever witnessed, but for giving me the opportunity to support Tottenham Hotspur Football Club. Come on you Spurs!

Stewart Peters

Gary Lineker with the FA Cup Spurs won in 1991.

Classic Matches

Tottenham Hotspur 3–2 West Herts	13 October 1894	FA Cup First Qualifying Round
Tottenham Hotspur 4–1 Notts County	4 September 1899	Friendly
Tottenham Hotspur 2–2 Sheffield United	20 April 1901	FA Cup final
Tottenham Hotspur 3–1 Sheffield United	27 April 1901	FA Cup final replay
Tottenham Hotspur 3–0 Wolverhampton Wanderers	1 September 1908	Football League Second Division
Tottenham Hotspur 1–0 Wolverhampton Wanderers	23 April 1921	FA Cup final
Tottenham Hotspur 5–5 Huddersfield Town	19 September 1925	Football League First Division
Tottenham Hotspur 4–3 Everton	27 February 1937	FA Cup fifth round replay
Tottenham Hotspur 7–0 Newcastle United	18 November 1950	Football League First Division
Tottenham Hotspur 1–0 Sheffield Wednesday	28 April 1951	Football League First Division
Tottenham Hotspur 10–4 Everton	11 October 1958	Football League First Division
Tottenham Hotspur 13–2 Crewe Alexandra	3 February 1960	FA Cup fourth round replay
Tottenham Hotspur 2–1 Sheffield Wednesday	17 April 1961	Football League First Division
Tottenham Hotspur 2–0 Leicester City	6 May 1961	FA Cup final
Tottenham Hotspur 8–1 Gornik Zabrze	20 September 1961	European Cup prel. rd 2nd leg
Tottenham Hotspur 2–1 Benfica	5 April 1962	European Cup semi-final 2nd leg
Tottenham Hotspur 3–1 Burnley	5 May 1962	FA Cup final
Tottenham Hotspur 5–1 Atletico Madrid	16 May 1963	European Cup Winners Cup final
Tottenham Hotspur 5–5 Aston Villa	19 March 1966	Football League First Division
Tottenham Hotspur 2–1 Chelsea	9 May 1967	FA Cup final
Tottenham Hotspur 2–0 Aston Villa	27 February 1971	League Cup final
Tottenham Hotspur 1–1 Wolverhampton Wanderers	17 May 1972	UEFA Cup final 2nd leg
Tottenham Hotspur 1–0 Norwich City	3 March 1973	League Cup final
Tottenham Hotspur 2–2 Feyenoord	21 May 1974	UEFA Cup final 1st leg
Tottenham Hotspur 4–2 Leeds United	28 April 1975	Football League First Division

Tottenham Hotspur 9–0 Bristol Rovers	22 October 1977	Football League Second Division
Tottenham Hotspur 1–0 Manchester United	9 January 1980	FA Cup third round replay
Tottenham Hotspur 3–0 Wolverhampton Wanderers	15 April 1981	FA Cup semi-final replay
Tottenham Hotspur 3–2 Manchester City	14 May 1981	FA Cup final replay
Tottenham Hotspur 3–2 Chelsea	6 March 1982	FA Cup quarter-final
Tottenham Hotspur 1–3 Liverpool	13 March 1982	League Cup final
Tottenham Hotspur 1–0 Queens Park Rangers	27 May 1982	FA Cup final replay
Tottenham Hotspur 4–2 Feyenoord	19 October 1983	UEFA Cup second round 1st leg
Tottenham Hotspur 1–1 Anderlecht	25 May 1984	UEFA Cup final 2nd leg
Tottenham Hotspur 5–0 West Ham United	2 February 1987	League Cup fifth round replay
Tottenham Hotspur 2–3 Coventry City	16 May 1987	FA Cup final
Tottenham Hotspur 3–1 Arsenal	14 April 1991	FA Cup semi-final
Tottenham Hotspur 2–1 Nottingham Forest	18 May 1991	FA Cup final
Tottenham Hotspur 4–3 Sheffield Wednesday	20 August 1994	FA Premiership
Tottenham Hotspur 6–2 Southampton	1 March 1995	FA Cup fifth round replay
Tottenham Hotspur 2–1 Liverpool	11 March 1995	FA Cup quarter-final
Tottenham Hotspur 6–2 Wimbledon	2 May 1998	FA Premiership
Tottenham Hotspur 1–0 Barnsley	16 March 1999	FA Cup quarter-final
Tottenham Hotspur 1–0 Leicester City	21 March 1999	League Cup final
Tottenham Hotspur 2–1 Arsenal	7 November 1999	FA Premiership
Tottenham Hotspur 3–2 West Ham United	11 March 2001	FA Cup quarter-final
Tottenham Hotspur 3–5 Manchester United	29 September 2001	FA Premiership
Tottenham Hotspur 5–1 Chelsea	23 January 2002	League Cup semi-final 2nd leg
Tottenham Hotspur 1–2 Blackburn Rovers	24 February 2002	League Cup final
Tottenham Hotspur 0–0 Manchester United	4 January 2005	FA Premiership

TOTTENHAM HOTSPUR v. WEST HERTS

Date: 13 October 1894

Match title: FA Cup first qualifying round

Location: Northumberland Park

Attendance: 2,000

Tottenham Hotspur Football Club were born in 1882, underneath a gas lamp at the Park Lane end of what is now White Hart Lane. The club was to be known as the Hotspur Football Club and was formed by a group of local schoolboys keen to add a winter sport to the already established Hotspur Cricket Club. The club was given the name 'Hotspur' in honour of Henry Percy, alias 'Harry Hotspur', who was a fierce, impulsive warrior who fought against the Scots and the French in the fourteenth century. He was a man who, together with his father, the 1st Earl of Northumberland, helped depose King Richard II from the throne in 1399. In addition, the Percy family owned a family seat on Tottenham Marshes, thus the link between the area and the legend.

The first recorded game featuring this fledgling Spurs club came in September 1882, where the youngsters were beaten 2–0 by another local side, The Radicals. The club were in need of some initial guidance. In August 1883, the boys approached Mr John Ripsher – an ironworks clerk and a man who had been involved with the running of the cricket club – to help out. Ripsher agreed to take on the role and the club became properly organised, with their games to be played on Tottenham Marshes, one of the many open spaces of land available in the area at the time. The club's first colours were navy blue. Having been renamed Tottenham Hotspur Football and Athletic Club at the end of the 1884/85 season so as to avoid confusion with the also established London Hotspur, Spurs achieved many firsts in those early years, including their first competitive match (a 5–2 thumping of London-based St Albans in the London Association Cup), a first change of official club colours (switching to blue and white halves in honour of FA Cup-winning Blackburn Rovers) and a first ever meeting with Arsenal (then Royal Arsenal), with Spurs leading 2–1 until the game was halted fifteen minutes from time due to diminishing light.

It was in 1888 when the team really began to take off. Crowds were coming in their thousands to the Marshes as Spurs' reputation for fine football and exciting, entertaining play began to blossom, and it soon became obvious that they were going to require a new home where they could profit from the watching public. A site was found at nearby Northumberland Park and, for a rental price of £10 per season, Spurs had themselves a new ground, shared initially with another club, Foxes F.C.

Spurs had risen steadily from a group of schoolboys just wanting to play to a promising, ever-improving force in the London area. In October 1894, a real milestone was reached as the club prepared to host its first ever FA Cup match – a first round qualifying tie. The opponents for the club's first venture into a competition with which they would become inextricably linked throughout their history were West Herts, a side that played in the nearby Watford area, and a club noted for their attacking flair.

Although the crowds that came to Northumberland Park in the early days were down on the number that used to watch on the Marshes (it was free to view at the latter), the 2,000 spectators watching the tie from the compact ground were treated to a game of free-flowing, highly entertaining football, traits that would become synonymous with Tottenham Hotspur and the FA Cup.

It seemed that Spurs were set to pummel their visitors as, in the first half, fine wing play from Ernie Payne – signed the previous season in controversial circumstances from Fulham – terrorised the visiting defence. It was

Tottenham Hotspur 3	West Herts 2
Hunter, Goodall,	Wright,
Cubberley	Hobbs

Payne's work that led to goals for Peter Hunter and Donald Goodall; Spurs went into the break brimming with confidence.

Just as Spurs began to envision an easy passage into the second qualifying round, they were given a rude awakening. Barely five minutes after the start of the second half, Wright scored for West Herts before Hobbs raced through to equalise, shocking the home side and their supporters. From there on, it appeared there would be only one winner, as West Herts poured forward in wave after wave of attack. Yet the Spurs rearguard held firm and, against the run of play, they forced a breakaway. Goodall brought the ball upfield and, slicing the West Herts defence open, released Archie Cubberley who, with total calm, slotted the ball past the despairing King in the West Herts goal. Cubberley's strike seemed to demoralise the visitors totally, and Spurs were unlucky not to add to their tally when forward Eccles' shot appeared to go under the crossbar. But with no nets in the goals the referee, Mr Bisiter, pointed for a goal kick to West Herts, hardly endearing himself to the angered home support.

It mattered not in the end, Spurs had won and had made a successful beginning to their FA Cup story. More joy followed in the second and third qualifying rounds before Luton Town ended their run in the fourth qualifying round, winning a replay 4–0.

It was the match against West Herts and the subsequent cup run that led the thinkers at Spurs to believe professionalism must be adopted. This would be necessary in order for the club to progress further and attain the league status they had harboured hopes of acquiring for some time (at this point the majority of the club's games were friendlies). The Football Association had accepted professionalism in 1885 and the Football League was formed in 1888. Many clubs in the Midlands and the North were already professional and the now 'Woolwich' Arsenal had become the first London club to turn professional. The likes of Millwall Athletic, Luton Town, Reading and Southampton St Marys had all followed suit from the South and Spurs were eager not to miss out. At a meeting in 1895, Spurs adopted professionalism and in 1896 a then-record crowd of 6,000 turned up at Northumberland Park to see the team play Aston Villa. It was that type of occasion that helped the club tremendously and, with their reputation continuing to grow, the club were voted into the First Division of the Southern League for the 1896/97 season, finally giving them the league football they craved. To celebrate their new status, the club again changed their official colours, this time to a highly tasteful chocolate and gold strip.

Tottenham Hotspur: Monk, Jull, Welham, Shepherd, Briggs, Julian, Cubberley, Goodall, Hunter, Eccles, Payne

West Herts: King, Lidderdale, Paul, Penney, Robbins, Green, Wright, Hobbs, Anderson, Taylor, Strout

TOTTENHAM HOTSPUR v. NOTTS COUNTY

Date: 4 September 1899

Location: White Hart Lane

Match title: Friendly

Attendance: 5,000

Spurs had made a decent start to life as a Southern League club, finishing fourth in the 1896/97 season as well as making an appearance (which they lost) in their first ever cup final – the local Wellinborough Charity Cup. Although they had adapted well to the physical demands of playing regular games in the Southern League and various other competitions, the financial status of the club needed improving. In stepped Charles Roberts, a trooper in the Herts Yeomanry and something of a wizard with regards to finances and raising funds. It was one of Roberts' first suggestions that Spurs became a limited company, reasoning that supporters and local businessman would relish the chance to own shares in a team that they could then truly call their own. From 2 March 1898, Spurs became a limited company and, although financial results were disappointing to begin with, they did improve, resulting in Spurs being able to attract players of higher value and superior ability to the club.

At the same time in 1898, Spurs appointed their first ever manager, Frank Bretell, who also held the role of club secretary. Originating from Liverpool, Bretell had played for Everton and joined Spurs having been prised away from the clutches of Bolton Wanderers. He already had the likes of Welshman John Jones – the club's first ever international player – in his ranks and, in the summer of 1898, with on-the-field results improving all the time, he was able to sign some high-quality players such as right-back Harry Erentz, half-back James McNaught, blazing-fast right-winger Tom Smith and the exciting centre forward John Cameron. At the end of the 1898/99 season, Bretell left his managerial position at Spurs to join Portsmouth and he was replaced as boss by one of the players he had signed for Spurs, John Cameron. As well as being manager and club secretary, Cameron would remain a key part of the playing team, but he was clearly unsatisfied with Spurs' efforts of the previous season (they finished seventh in the Southern League) and he began to recruit a whole host of talented individuals to take Spurs further along their road to success. Among those who Cameron persuaded to join were goalkeeper George Clawley, steely, reliable defenders Sandy Tait and Ted Hughes, never-say-die half-back Tom Morris, thrilling, attack-minded players in David Copeland and John Kirwan, and goal-scorer extraordinaire Tom Pratt. It was around this group of stars that the first great Spurs side was built. In what was proving a hectic and thoroughly eventful season, Charles Roberts also took over as club chairman, the team changed their official colours to blue and white and – most significant historically – moved into a new ground.

Two years previously, with the club's status growing rapidly, some 14,000 fans had crammed dangerously into Northumberland Park to watch the team's game with rivals Woolwich Arsenal. Almost 100 people had clambered onto the roof of a refreshment bar seeking a better view of the match. Not surprisingly, the building – unprepared for such an onslaught – collapsed, with tragedy narrowly avoided. The incident provided Spurs with a warning that, if they wanted to progress both on and off the field, a new ground would be a necessity. Behind the White Hart Pub in Tottenham High Road lay a patch of land formerly used as a market garden that had been obtained by brewers Charringtons. Charles Roberts agreed with both Charringtons and the landlord of the plot that Spurs would lease the ground and thus the plot became Tottenham's new home. The new ground – to which Spurs moved some of the stands from Northumberland Park – was originally to be named Gilpin Park,

Tottenham Hotspur 4	Notts County 1
Pratt,	McCairns
Copeland (3)	

TOTTENHAM HOTSPUR v. NOTTS COUNTY

John Cameron.

but with that title never actually made official, the ground eventually became known as White Hart Lane, which to this day remains the world-famous home of the Spurs.

In September 1899, and still non-league, Spurs opened the gates at White Hart Lane for the first time for a friendly against a powerhouse from the Football League First Division. Notts County were a club with a reputation for hard-nosed, no-nonsense football. With the exception of John Jones, every player who played for Spurs that day had either been signed by Frank Bretell or John Cameron, and it would not take long for the football world to discover that this new-look, enterprising and eye-catching Spurs side was a team on the rise. With chairman Charles Roberts having conducted the pre-match ceremony, the 5,000 fans inside White Hart Lane settled down in the September sunshine to watch a most entertaining encounter. Physical and direct, Notts County scored first when a long ball found McCairns, who beat Clawley in the Spurs goal. But Spurs were soon passing the ball around briskly and efficiently, with their attacking play most pleasing to watch. The tricky wingers Smith and Kirwan severely tested the First Division side's defence, linking up in some sweeping moves with forwards Pratt, Copeland and Cameron. Spurs were rewarded for their endeavour moments before half-time when Kirwan – the game's outstanding player on the left wing, sent over a cross that was thumped into the County net by Pratt, lifting Tottenham's spirits going into the break. Coming out flying at the start of the second half, Spurs took the game to County. Pratt had a shot blocked by Suter, the visitors' goalkeeper, but the ball rebounded to inside left David Copeland, and the Scot made no mistake to make it 2–1 to Spurs. After an hour, Suter had to leave the field through injury and so Bull – normally a midfielder – went in goal for County (there were no substitutes in this era of football). Naturally, the advantage now lay with Spurs, and with their craft and work-rate inspiring, Copeland was able to score twice more, giving him the first ever White Hart Lane hat-trick and presenting Spurs with a debut win at their new home. This performance was followed up a week later when Spurs won the first league game at the Lane, a 1–0 Southern League victory over QPR, watched by an encouraging crowd of 11,000.

It may well have only been a friendly, but the match with Notts County was a very important game in the history of the club. The historical reasons are obvious but, in football terms, the match proved that Spurs could compete with the best sides in the land. Over the next few seasons, this first great Spurs side would proudly go on to achieve one of the finest moments in the history of Tottenham Hotspur.

Tottenham Hotspur: Clawley, Erentz, Tait, Jones, McNaught, Morris, Smith, Pratt, Copeland, Cameron, Kirwan

Notts County: Sutter, Lewis, Montgomery, Ball, Bull, Lowe, Hadlei, MacConachie, McCairns, Fletcher, Chalmers

TOTTENHAM HOTSPUR v. SHEFFIELD UNITED

Date: 20 April 1901

Location: Crystal Palace

Match title: FA Cup final

Attendance: 110,820

The 1899/00 season began with Southampton as rock-solid favourites to record a fourth consecutive title in the Southern League. But it was Spurs that came shooting out of the blocks like a hungry cheetah, winning their first thirteen games and playing some fine football in the process. By the turn of the year, Spurs were one of three clubs (Southampton and Portsmouth were the others) that held a realistic chance of winning the league. When Southampton's league form dipped because of a run to the final of the FA Cup, Spurs found themselves involved in a head-to-head battle with Portsmouth, managed of course by Frank Bretell.

Spurs had beaten Portsmouth convincingly, 3–1, on Christmas Day 1899, but had suffered a 1–0 defeat to their rivals the following March, a result that kept the South Coast club right in the mix of the title challenge to the death. But Spurs had enough resolve and extra attacking flair to hold off the challenge and, when they won 2–1 away to New Brompton in the final game of the season, a first ever championship, albeit a non-league one, was theirs. It had been a wonderful campaign for Spurs, only losing four league games to emerge as the top team in the South of the country outside the Football League. For the 1900/01 campaign, manager John Cameron was dealt a blow when prolific marksman Tom Pratt – scorer of an incredible 54 goals the previous season – revealed he was unhappy living in the South and requested a transfer. Pratt was reluctantly allowed to leave Spurs to join Preston North End, the club from which he had joined Tottenham. His goals and general presence were certain to be missed back at White Hart Lane, and a capable replacement had to be found. True, Cameron and David Copeland had performed as principal centre forwards in their time, but the pair had become intrinsic to Spurs' inter-linking, close-passing game as inside forwards. Cameron signed the highly talented Scot Sandy Brown from Portsmouth to take Pratt's place.

With the defence of their Southern League crown proving somewhat disappointing, it was the FA Cup that was to help take Tottenham's progress to new, glorious heights. Injuries to key players had affected the form of the side in their league play, and the start of the FA Cup was delayed until the end of February because of the death of Queen Victoria, an episode that had left the country in shock and in a state of mourning, bringing the nation to a complete standstill. King Edward VII succeeded Queen Victoria on the throne.

When the first round of the competition finally took place, Spurs faced a tough game against First Division Preston North End, and their former striker Pratt, at White Hart Lane. Pratt proved on the day that he was more than capable of rising above any sentiment he may have had for his former team, displaying his wonderful talent and being central to all that was good in Preston's attacking play. Spurs must have wished they still had the hitman in their ranks as his successor, Sandy Brown, was playing poorly, clumsily wasting a number of chances. It looked bleak for Spurs as they trailed 1–0 until, with just nine minutes to go, a cross from Kirwan was forced home by none other than Brown, gratefully salvaging Spurs a replay. The replay took place just four days later at Deepdale before a porous crowd of just 6,000. The equalising goal in the first match was perhaps the catalyst for both Sandy Brown's Spurs career and Tottenham's long-lasting love affair with the FA Cup. From that moment onwards, the Scot fully portrayed his excellence as a premier centre forward and, in a surprisingly soft replay,

Tottenham Hotspur 2	Sheffield United 2
Brown (2)	Priest,
	Bennett

Tottenham Hotspur v. Sheffield United

A huge crowd at Crystal Palace Stadium watch the 1901 FA Cup final.

Spurs easily beat Preston 4–2, with Brown notching a hat-trick and Cameron adding the other. The FA Cup run had begun. Another First Division side, FA Cup holders Bury, were disposed of 2–1 at White Hart Lane in the second round with Brown scoring both and, after a rough-and-tumble third round tie at Reading had finished level at 1–1 (Kirwan scoring for Spurs), a Brown double and a single strike from Copeland (who had been one of Tottenham's early season injury casualties) in the replay sent Spurs through to a semi-final match with West Bromwich Albion.

The semi-final was to take place at Villa Park, making it a far closer and convenient venue for the players and supporters of Albion than those from Tottenham. Even so, the Spurs fans did their side proud, attending the match in their masses, so much so that the bulk of the 46,000 crowd were from London. On the day, the team repaid their fans' support, demonstrating superior speed and skill and running out convincing 4–0 winners. The outstanding figure of Brown scored all four. Non-league Spurs had incredibly made it through to an FA Cup final, yet the authority of much of their play – especially in the replay with Preston and the game against Bury – led many to believe that they were more than capable of actually winning the cup.

Their opponents in the final were First Division Sheffield United, a team that had won the league in 1898 and the FA Cup a year later. In the United side were such high-class performers as wing half Ernest Needham, forward Fred Priest – who had scored in three FA Cup finals – and certainly the most recognisable figure of the

---

Tottenham Hotspur: Clawley, Erentz, Tait, Morris, Hughes, Jones, Smith, Cameron, Brown, Copeland, Kirwan

Sheffield United: Foulke, Thickett, Boyle, Johnson, Morren, Needham, Bennett, Field, Hedley, Priest, Lipsham

Tottenham Hotspur v. Sheffield United

Sandy Brown has just scored for Spurs as 'Fatty' Foulke goes to retrieve the ball.

1901 final, the extraordinarily large goalkeeper, Bill 'Fatty' Foulke, unquestionably the heaviest player in the professional game at the time. A record crowd in excess of 110,000 flocked to Crystal Palace for the final, with many of the Sheffield United fans travelling down to London from Yorkshire by train, and the surging swell of supporters and cries of excited voices – many of whom packed in to the stadium hours before kick-off – lent great enthusiasm and immense atmosphere to the occasion. Interestingly, the 1901 cup final was the first to be recorded on film, and that fact would have been greatly beneficial when reviewing the key moment of the game when it was over.

Playing in their first FA Cup final, Spurs understandably showed some nervousness early on in the match, and it was United that dictated the initial portion of the game. However, it was not long before the neat, quick and effective football that had pioneered Spurs' run to the final came to life. The strong half-back line of Tom Morris, captain John Jones and centre half Ted Hughes (who had come into the side for the injured James McNaught for the Preston replay and had held his place ever since) began to control the play, presenting Tottenham's forward line with a number of chances to break the deadlock. They very nearly did, when smart play between Copeland and Kirwan allowed Brown to slide a pass through to Cameron but, just as the player-manager was bearing down on goal, the flag was raised for offside. However it was to be United that took the lead when, after twelve minutes, a twenty-yard shot from Priest beat the despairing dive of Clawley in the Spurs goal, sending the northern fans into raptures. But Spurs soon seized back control, passing the ball around swiftly and after twenty-five minutes a long-range free-kick was met with a firm header by Brown, levelling the scores, and ensuring that the Scot had scored in every round of the FA Cup. Both goalkeepers were kept busy in a lively final, and the tall, angular Clawley was forced into some acrobatics to keep United at bay, while the considerably wider Foulke proved a capable barrier at the other end. It was to be Spurs that went ahead for the first time five minutes into the second half. The goal was a thing of beauty involving half the Spurs team. Welshman Jones sent Kirwan away down the left wing, the Irishman then releasing Cameron to run at goal. With the United defence drawn to the Spurs inside right, Brown found himself free in the box and when Cameron picked him out with an inch-perfect pass, the striker was able to shoot fiercely past Foulke and put Spurs 2–1 up.

Given the football Spurs had shown up to that point, it looked likely that the Londoners would go on and record a handsome victory. But United were tough, experienced and resolute, and incredibly were level just a minute later, although the goal reeked of foul play and provided an incident of huge controversy. When the left-sided forward Bert Lipsham shot with some power, Clawley could only parry the attempt and, with the ball trickling slowly towards the Spurs goal-line, United forward Walter Bennett rushed in to try and bundle the ball home. Frantically, Clawley was able to push the ball away for a corner and Spurs believed they had escaped a seriously dangerous moment. The linesman accordingly signalled for a corner but, to the horror of the Spurs players and their fans, referee Mr Kingscott pointed to the centre circle and Sheffield United had been gifted a most fortunate equaliser. The crowd reaction was unanimous in their disapproval of the decision, and Mr Kingscott was jeered and harassed for the remainder of the game, in which Spurs appeared to lose their concentration and had to defend for long periods to deny United a winner.

It had been a thrilling, if controversial cup final, and of course, the main talking point was Sheffield United's 'phantom' second goal. There could not have been a more perfect time for the beginning of filmed football, as the footage later proved that the ball had been nowhere near crossing the line and that Mr Kingscott had indeed been incorrect in his decision by an embarrassing margin. Despite their hard luck, Spurs had acquitted themselves with great credit in their first cup final and were determined to see justice done in the replay the following Saturday.

Tottenham Hotspur v. Sheffield United

Date: 27 April 1901

Location: Burnden Park, Bolton

Match title: FA Cup final replay

Attendance: 20,470

Originally, the replay for the 1901 cup final was to take place at Goodison Park, home of Everton. However, Merseyside neighbours Liverpool were involved in a league match on the same day and complained about the final taking place in such close proximity. Therefore, it was Bolton's ground, Burnden Park, that was selected to host the much-anticipated replay, with the Lancashire venue expected to attract a big gate. It was bitterly disappointing for all concerned when the attendance was a mere one-fifth the size of the encounter at Crystal Palace, only just topping 20,000. Much of the blame was placed on the shoulders of the railway company responsible for Lancashire and Yorkshire trains, who refused to offer special low-rate fares for those wishing to make the long journey up from London.

Neither side changed their line-ups from those that had contested the first game, and it was Spurs that started the brighter in their quest to achieve the victory they believed was rightfully theirs. For all that Spurs were dominating possession – the half-back line of Morris, Hughes and Jones again impressing – attempts at the Sheffield United goal were few and far between, with 'Fatty' Foulke rarely troubled. In fact, it was to be United that struck the first blow when, just five minutes before the interval, good work involving Needham and Lipsham set up a chance for Priest, who confidently drilled the ball past Clawley to give the Yorkshire side the lead, just as he had in the first game. Never wavering from their own brand of free-flowing football, Spurs attacked with vigour at the start of the second half. Priest's goal late in the first half had served as a wake-up call to the Southern League side, and they now set about laying siege to the Sheffield goal.

Foulke had already been called in to action a number of times when a crisp exchange of passes between Brown and Copeland set up John Cameron in space, and the player-manager brought roars from the crowd as he sent a powerful long-range shot past the goalkeeper for the equaliser. It was a trademark strike from Cameron, whose fine ability to run with the ball and his great technical skill often saw him carve open shooting opportunities for himself, and he was a regular on the scoresheet in Tottenham games, despite moving from his early career position of central striker to inside forward.

Sheffield United, though still very much in the game, were now under serious pressure, and a mistake at the back allowed Tom Smith to pounce on a loose ball and put Spurs 2–1 ahead. Normally more adept at setting up goals with his dangerous right-wing crosses, the lightning-quick Smith found himself in the right place at the right time to give Tottenham a grip on the cup that they would never loosen. Having scored in every round of the cup, Sandy Brown rose to meet a corner seven minutes from time and, as his accurate header nestled in the back of the United net, the cup was bound for Tottenham. As the final whistle blew, those fans that had made the journey from London cheered their team with sheer delight as Spurs won the FA Cup for the first time.

Captain John Jones was to be the first man in club history to get his hands on the FA Cup, proudly receiving the trophy from Lord Kinnaird. John Cameron could take great pleasure in the triumph having assembled and added much of the team to the one that Frank Bretell had begun to put in place. However, the real star of the 1901 FA Cup story was Scottish centre forward Sandy Brown. The Scot had scored in every round, netting a

Tottenham Hotspur 3	Sheffield United 1
Cameron, Smith, Brown	Priest

TOTTENHAM HOTSPUR *v.* SHEFFIELD UNITED

Tom Morris takes a throw-in during the replay.

remarkable fifteen goals in total. He only played for Spurs for one more season and then had stints with Portsmouth and Middlesbrough, but he will forever be recognised as one of the first true heroes of Tottenham Hotspur Football Club.

So Spurs had become the first – and to date only – team from outside the Football League to win the FA Cup, a feat that, given the way football has evolved in England since 1901, will surely never be repeated. In turn, Spurs brought much-needed glory and attention to football in the South, which at the time was certainly held in lesser regard than the game in the North. This batch of Tottenham players made up the first great side the club produced and, unknowingly, they also started a fine tradition of success for Spurs when the year ended in '1'.

Tottenham Hotspur: Clawley, Erentz, Tait, Morris, Hughes, Jones, Smith, Cameron, Brown, Copeland, Kirwan

Sheffield United: Foulke, Thickett, Boyle, Johnson, Morren, Needham, Bennett, Field, Hedley, Priest, Lipsham

TOTTENHAM HOTSPUR v. WOLVERHAMPTON WANDERERS

Date: 1 September 1908

Location: White Hart Lane

Match title: Football League Second Division

Attendance: 20,000

Beginning in March 1907, Tottenham Hotspur would experience a series of changes that altered the standing of the club and thrust its direction into a new era of progress. It was at this time that John Cameron, long associated with Spurs both as a fine forward and highly regarded manager, resigned, somewhat surprisingly. It transpired that Cameron had suffered a number of disagreements with fellow directors at the club. In his place came Fred Kirkham. Kirkham's was a reign that was not greatly appreciated by the Spurs supporters and, unable to bring further success to Tottenham, he was to prove unpopular with players and directors alike, eventually leaving before the start of the 1908 season. Kirkham's time at the club seemed to perfectly illustrate the predicament in which Spurs found themselves. As a team capable of holding their own against the best sides in the land and being in a geographical location primed to gather a large fan base, the Southern League seemed not to meet the ambition of the club. With the Football League progressing from strength to strength, it appeared Spurs were in danger of being left behind.

In early 1908 Spurs chairman Charles Roberts revealed Tottenham would be attempting to gain election to the Football League for the following season's play, a move also made by Bradford (strangely a Southern League side) and Queens Park Rangers. The Southern League reacted with menace to the proposals from their members, expelling both Spurs and QPR, while Bradford resigned. All this meant that Spurs were now in an all-or-nothing situation, with commitment totally aimed at winning election to the Football League. Spurs were one of six clubs seeking election but, at a Football League meeting, Chesterfield, Grimsby Town and Bradford received the majority of the votes, leaving Spurs in a desperate football wilderness with no league football at all. With only two divisions in the Football League and no plans for a third, and having been expelled from the Southern League, Tottenham Hotspur had reached a crossroads in their history. Then arrived a glimmer of hope.

Stoke City had been relegated to the Football League Second Division and soon claimed the attendances they would get in that division would not generate sufficient money for their survival, so they resigned. Therefore, one place was now vacant in the Second Division, and a further meeting was called in June 1908 where Spurs, Lincoln, Southport, Rotherham Town and Stoke – who had since changed their mind and decided they wanted to compete after all – were the five clubs seeking election. An initial vote saw Southport, Rotherham Town and Stoke eliminated and when a second call saw the forty votes on offer split evenly between Spurs and Lincoln, the decision was referred to the Football League management committee. The glorious news soon arrived that Spurs had won a deciding vote 5–3, a scoreline as significant as any match that had preceded that moment, and a place in the Football League Second Division was theirs. From that moment onwards, Tottenham Hotspur would remain a Football League club. As if to rub salt in the wounds of Stoke, Spurs signed three of their players, adding to a squad that at last had the opportunity to display their exciting talents on the biggest stage in the land on a consistent basis. Among those players were Tom Morris, the lone holdover from the 1901 cup-winning team, and Vivian John Woodward, Tottenham's undisputed star and one of the best players of his era. An outstanding centre forward, Woodward had spent most of the early part of the century at the club and,

Tottenham Hotspur 3	Wolverhampton Wanderers 0
Woodward (2),	
Morris	

Tottenham Hotspur v. Wolverhampton Wanderers

Vivian Woodward.

as an international, scored 29 goals for England between 1903 and 1911, including four in a match against Austria before the start of Tottenham's first Football League campaign. A fine cricketer too, Woodward normally joined up with his teammates when that particular season was over but, on the announcement that Spurs had been elected to the Football League, Woodward stated that he would be with Spurs from day one of the inaugural season.

Assuming Stoke's fixtures, Tottenham's first game in league football was against the holders of the FA Cup and one of the longest-serving Football League clubs, Wolverhampton Wanderers. Wolves were fancied to teach the league new-boys an early lesson. As it transpired, it was to be Spurs that performed the teaching, dominating the game from the start, proving that the brand of football that had made them such a popular draw in the Southern League could win them plenty of games – as well as countless new supporters nationwide – in the Football League itself.

Barely six minutes had elapsed when Woodward became the first man to score a goal for Spurs in the Football League. Lunn in the Wolves goal saved a free-kick from winger Joe Walton and there was Woodward to stab home the rebound and put Spurs 1–0 up. Tottenham's rearguard, featuring full-backs Burton and Couquet and marshalled by the evergreen Morris, were admirably keeping the Wolves attack in check, limiting the visitors to one dangerous moment when Radford had the ball in the back of the net only for the goal to be disallowed for offside.

It was Spurs that came out for the second half in attacking mode, and a second Woodward goal arrived shortly after. Despite Wolves' attempt to claw their way back in to the match, Tom Morris capped a dream league start for Spurs by blasting home a long-range effort to make the final score 3–0. The result set the standard for the remainder of the season. From 38 league games, Spurs won 20 and lost just 7 and in the process scored 67 goals. It was enough to give them second place in the table, finishing ahead of West Bromwich Albion on goal difference, and sensationally winning the club promotion at the first attempt, rising to the First Division together with Bolton Wanderers. In the First Division Spurs stayed (without any great success) until they finished bottom in the 1914/15 season. The Football League was then put on hold until 1919 because of the First World War and, when it reconvened, Spurs found themselves in the Second Division amid most controversial circumstances as a result of some most foul play from the club that would become their fiercest rivals, Arsenal.

Tottenham Hotspur: Hewitson, Couquet, Burton, Morris, D. Steel, Darnell, Walton, Woodward, McFarlane, R. Steel, Middlemiss

Wolverhampton Wanderers: Lunn, Jones, Collins, Hunt, Woolridge, Bishop, Harrison, Shelton, Hadley, Radford, Pedley

TOTTENHAM HOTSPUR v. WOLVERHAMPTON WANDERERS

Date: 23 April 1921

Location: Stamford Bridge

Match title: FA Cup final

Attendance: 72,805

At the end of the 1914/15 season, Spurs had finished dead last in the twenty-team First Division, a single point behind the only other Southern-based side in the division, Chelsea. After the season was over, all Football League fixtures were suspended because of the First World War, and the league did not reconvene until 1919.

For the 1919/20 season, the Football League had decided to increase the number of teams in the First Division to twenty-two. The last time this had happened, in 1905, the two teams that had finished at the bottom of the First Division – Bury and Notts County – were allowed to stay up because of the increase, so it was reasonable thinking for Spurs to assume the same treatment. How wrong Spurs were. Having not long moved to a new ground called Highbury (which was very close to Tottenham's north London home White Hart Lane), Arsenal – who had finished fifth in the Second Division in the last pre-war season – campaigned that it should be them and not Spurs that took the twenty-second and final place in the First Division on grounds that they had been established as a Football League club longer than Spurs. In one of the most controversial and unfair decisions in Football League history (led by league president John McKenna – a close friend of the Arsenal chairman Henry Norris), a meeting in 1919 saw Arsenal voted to the First Division and Spurs condemned to the Second.

Quite understandably, the decision appalled Tottenham, yet all was not lost. They had been steadily building a young side ever since manager Peter McWilliam – a former player with Newcastle and Scotland – had been appointed manager in 1913. The Spurs players who had not enlisted for service in the First World War had played in the London Football Combination during those years, and were gelling and progressing all the time.

Of course, the real test for McWilliam's side would be when the league action began again in 1919, but any doubts concerning the new-look Tottenham team were emphatically quashed as the club blitzed the Second Division, winning it with a record number of points – 70 (two points for a win) – and scoring an incredible 102 league goals in the process, as they marched straight back to the top flight.

Such was the authority of their season-long performance the year before that Spurs were earmarked as a side to watch for the 1920/21 season. There was never the slightest indication during that campaign in the First Division that Spurs would struggle, and they eventually finished sixth (three places higher than Arsenal), all the time exhibiting their blossoming attacking play, scoring 88 goals in their league and cup matches as the players from White Hart Lane developed into the finest Tottenham side since the cup-winning team of 1901.

Bill Jacques, a signing from Coventry City six years previously, was the goalkeeper and was one of the best of his era, although he got injured and was replaced by Alex Hunter in February 1921. Tommy Clay, the captain and a man who would play fifteen years for Spurs, led a defence that included the ever-improving left-back Bob McDonald and centre half Charlie Walters – a defender who would not have looked out of place in the modern day Italian Serie A, such was his hard-nosed, no-nonsense style. Walters' emergence meant that Spurs had the luxury of releasing one of the long-time defensive stalwarts, Charlie Rance.

Bert Smith was the man who did the dirty work in the half-back line; working tirelessly to win possession and set up attacks, while opposite him was one of the finest players in Spurs history, Arthur Grimsdell. Replacing

Tottenham Hotspur 1

Dimmock

Wolverhampton Wanderers 0

TOTTENHAM HOTSPUR v. WOLVERHAMPTON WANDERERS

The 1921 cup-winning team. Back row from left to right; Billy Minter (trainer), Clay, Smith, Hunter, Walters, McDonald. Front row from left to right; Banks, Seed, Grimsdell, Cantrell, Bliss, Dimmock.

Clay as skipper during the season, Grimsdell had everything needed in his game to make him a star of the era; strength, skill, tackling and passing ability as well as a deadly strike from all distances. He was at the centre of all that was effective for this Spurs side, and went on to captain England on three occasions as well as playing for Spurs until 1929.

It was, however, the five-man forward line that really whetted the appetite for Spurs fans. Twenty-year-old left-winger Jimmy Dimmock quickly became a fan favourite for his close skills and ability to attack defenders with pace and precision, while Jimmy Banks and the diminutive Fanny Walden (who was injured halfway through the season) provided excellent service on the opposite flank. Bert Bliss played inside left and was a player who scored many goals with his tendency to shoot at every opportunity, while at inside right was Jimmy Seed, a beautifully gifted creator and craftsman who linked the forward play together immaculately. Last but not least was the veteran of the side, thirty-eight-year-old centre forward Jimmy Cantrell. Similar in style to Teddy

---

Tottenham Hotspur: Hunter, Clay, McDonald, Smith, Walters, Grimsdell, Banks, Seed, Cantrell, Bliss, Dimmock

Wolverhampton Wanderers: George, Woodward, Marshall, Gregory, Hodnett, Riley, Lea, Burrill, Edmonds, Potts, Brooks

Tottenham Hotspur v. Wolverhampton Wanderers

Sheringham of modern years, Cantrell's quick brain not only saw him score plenty of goals but also provided many for his teammates.

It was the FA Cup that was again to be the highlight of the season and provide another wonderful chapter in the history of Tottenham Hotspur. Bristol Rovers were easily disposed of, 6–2 at White Hart Lane in the first round, and Bradford City were beaten just as comfortably, 4–0 at home in round two.

Spurs were then drawn away to Third Division Southend United in round three and soon found themselves in a real hole, 1–0 down after an hour of play. They then stepped up their attacking play considerably, blitzing their hosts with four killer goals, three from Seed, meaning he had scored in every round so far.

A huge crowd of over 50,000 turned up at White Hart Lane for the quarter-final with cup holders Aston Villa and the Spurs supporters went home in jubilant mood following a first-half strike from Jimmy Banks.

Jimmy Seed.

TOTTENHAM HOTSPUR v. WOLVERHAMPTON WANDERERS

The semi-final against Preston at Hillsborough turned out to be a largely one-sided affair and, although North End scored a consolation goal late on, Spurs had earlier struck through two Bert Bliss goals and their place in their second FA Cup final was assured.

Tottenham's opponents in the 1921 FA Cup final were Wolverhampton Wanderers, a side that had been struggling in the Second Division the past few seasons and had managed to get by Cardiff in the other semi-final. Spurs were clear favourites in the final, but the conditions that awaited Tottenham at Stamford Bridge on the day were far from ideal for their slick football. Torrential rain had turned the pitch into a virtual pond, with surface water and mud set to wreak havoc during the match.

Despite the atrocious weather, a colossal crowd of over 70,000 ploughed in to Stamford Bridge with some fans even taking up positions on the running track around the pitch so as to obtain a better view of the action.

Harsh winds meant the rain was literally driving into the players' faces and, fortunately for Spurs, it was they who won the coin toss, playing with the wind in the first half when the elements were at their most severe.

The first clear chance of the game fell to Bert Bliss, but his shot was hit straight at George in the Wolves goal, while another first-half opportunity – an acrobatic overhead kick from Bliss – was cleared off the line by the back-tracking Marshall, as the Second Division side frantically tried to hold on.

In truth, as much as Spurs tried to play their football, conditions were too much to cope with and, although Dimmock, Bliss and Grimsdell – the left side of the Spurs team – persevered admirably, the game was developing into a war of attrition.

Then came the breakthrough on fifty-five minutes. Right half Bert Smith broke from the back and attacked the Wolves defence before switching the play to Bliss on the left, who in turn released Dimmock through on goal in an instant. Trying to out-manoeuvre the Wolves right-back Woodward, Dimmock received a slice of luck when the ball came off the defender's leg and back into the Spurs man's path and, from there, Dimmock was able to slide a shot through the mud and into the net to give the London side the lead.

It was then that Charlie Walters rose to the occasion in the Spurs defence. As Wolves sprang to life, the defender put in some miraculous tackles including a goal-saving challenge on Brooks, who had the goal at his mercy. While at the other end, the likes of Seed, Cantrell and Banks had struggled all game for Spurs, Walters was truly outstanding at the back, and again robbed Wolves of an equaliser late on with a last-ditch tackle on their forward Potts.

As the final whistle was blown by Mr J. Davies, Spurs could finally celebrate a well earned but most gruelling of cup wins, and became the first team from the South to win the competition since they themselves had achieved the honour back in 1901. Although blunted for the most part in the final, the fantastic five-man forward line had been the stars of the cup run. In the competition, Seed had scored five goals, Bliss four, Banks three, Cantrell two with Dimmock grabbing the all-important strike in the final.

It would be the golden moment in a superb career at Spurs for Arthur Grimsdell, and as he received the cup from King George V, Spurs had again won the trophy when the year ended in '1'.

Tottenham Hotspur v. Huddersfield Town

Date: 19 September 1925

Location: White Hart Lane

Match title: Football League First Division

Attendance: 21,667

Under the excellent guidance of manager Peter McWilliam, Spurs had become a steady, successful force in the First Division. By now well renowned for their quick passing and slick attacking play, they had developed in to a fine side in the early 1920s. After their promotion from the Second Division, they had finished sixth in the First Division in 1920/21, finished runners-up to Liverpool a season later and had also recorded that memorable second FA Cup victory in 1921.

However, as the decade wore on, that great side of the early 1920s gradually began to break up. There remained some formidable talent at the club, such as the strong-tackling, quick-thinking right-back Tommy Clay, the aggressive and skilful mainstay Arthur Grimsdell, the 'brain' of the attack, Jimmy Seed and the wizard-like dribbling skills of the ever-popular Jimmy Dimmock.

But replacing players like Charlie Walters, Bert Bliss and Jimmy Cantrell had proved most difficult. In addition to problems at the back and at centre forward, the goalkeeping position was becoming a real headache for the team, as none of the multiple candidates the club tried proved to be the long-term solution.

The other problem for the team was the board of director's insistence on not splashing out top money to bring in new players. There were, however, a number of additions to the squad that proved positive. The first of these was inside forward Jack Elkes who joined from Southampton in 1923. Elkes was recognised as a good passer and dribbler from his midfield role, and was a player capable of scoring vital goals. The second of these useful signings was South African-born Frank Osborne, who arrived in January 1924. Osborne was basically a centre forward, but often he would play on the right wing, due to a lack of viable options in the position. Whether he was utilised on the wing or as the chief marksman, the talented Osborne regularly contributed his fair share of goals.

The 1925/26 season would prove to be something of a roller coaster campaign for Spurs. The team started the season well, and one of the most memorable games in club history arrived on 19 September 1925, when Spurs entertained Huddersfield Town, the reigning league champions and a side destined to win the title again in 1925/26.

Managed by future Arsenal boss Herbert Chapman, Huddersfield were a strong, physical side that opted for a direct approach, wasting no time in hurling long, dangerous balls into their opponents' penalty areas. Spurs on the other hand relied, as ever, on their swift and fluent passing game, and the two contrasting styles led to a fantastic game played in far from perfect conditions – the pitch was rain-soaked and slippery – rendering both defences prone to errors, and especially worrying for a Spurs side that had gone through six different goalkeepers in recent years.

The man between the posts on this day for Spurs was Fred Hinton, and he must have wondered if he was in the right profession as the away side played their part in a whirlwind beginning to the match, taking a 2–1 lead after just thirteen minutes – the Spurs goal scored by Elkes.

Slowly but surely, Spurs began to impose themselves on the champions and, in the second half, their endeavour was rewarded with goals from Dimmock and Clay, the latter from a penalty, to go 3–2 in front.

Tottenham Hotspur 5	Huddersfield Town 5
Elkes (2), Dimmock,	Jackson (4),
Clay (pen.), Osborne	Brown

TOTTENHAM HOTSPUR v. HUDDERSFIELD TOWN

Jimmy Dimmock.

The Huddersfield forward Jackson quickly equalised but Spurs responded by pouring forward in droves, and looked like scoring every time they attacked. They roared 5–3 ahead with two goals inside a minute from Osborne and Elkes.

Jimmy Seed – who had been at the heart of all that was good about Spurs on the day, linking up the forward play delightfully – was crudely knocked unconscious by a rough challenge later in the second half, and his loss turned the game upside down.

Showing the fight, determination and spirit that would make them dual champions, Huddersfield forced a fourth goal when Jackson scored late on. Then with just four minutes remaining, and Spurs hanging on grimly, the visitors got their equaliser through Brown as Spurs succumbed to the constant pressure brought about principally from the mismatch in numbers.

It finished five apiece and the 21,667 present applauded the players richly at the end having witnessed an incredible match. The game showed Spurs could rival the very best in the division with their restructured side, and by October they proudly sat atop the First Division.

However, it was indeed to be a season of ups and downs at Tottenham Hotspur. Their inspirational captain Arthur Grimsdell broke his leg at Leicester shortly after the team had climbed to the peak of the table, and from then on, Spurs' form plummeted alarmingly. With Grimsdell missing and the goalkeeping position still unresolved, Spurs conceded a whopping 79 goals in the league, by far the most since they had been promoted, and the forward line was never able to find the cohesion and continuity of the side of a few years previously. Tottenham finished the year in fifteenth place, thirteenth the season after and, when they ended the 1927/28 season ahead of only Middlesbrough – with manager Peter McWilliam now sadly departed having failed to see his ambitions matched by the directors – the club was relegated to the Second Division, where they would spend the next five seasons.

Tottenham Hotspur: Hinton, Clay, Forster, Skinner, Smith, Grimsdell, Osborne, Seed, Lindsay, Elkes, Dimmock

Huddersfield Town: Taylor, Barkas, Wadsworth, Steele, Wilson, Watson, Jackson, Cook, Brown, Stephenson, Williams

Tottenham Hotspur v. Everton

Date: 27 February 1937

Location: White Hart Lane

Match title: FA Cup fifth round replay

Attendance: 46,972

Having gained promotion to the First Division for the 1933/34 season, Spurs lasted only two years in the top flight until they disappointingly and most unexpectedly dropped down once more. Since being relegated again to the Second Division, Spurs had met something of a dead end. In the 1935/36 season, the club – who many had expected to gain instant promotion – had finished only seventh. In the 1936/37 campaign, they were fairing even worse in their league quest, floundering in mid-table come February, with no hope of bouncing back to the top division.

Percy Smith had been manager for the early part of the 1930s, yet he resigned when the team were relegated. In July 1935, it was Jack Tresadern's turn to manage the side, and hopes were high that the former West Ham captain could take the club up again. But as the team's league performances deteriorated woefully during Tresadern's first two seasons in charge, many Spurs fans wondered why the manager was not bringing in top-quality players to push the club forward. Tresadern, like a number of Spurs managers before him, was discovering that the board of directors were hesitant when it came to forking out top money, and so he had to be content with nurturing a number of talented homegrown players together with a sprinkling of new blood to try and improve matters. Among the homegrown players was locally born Arthur Rowe, who proved to be a key component in Tresadern's side. A graceful, footballing centre half, Rowe had first broken into the team in 1931 and had progressed to a point where Tottenham's performances were often far inferior in his absence. For example, when an injury during the Christmas period of 1934 sidelined him for a large chunk of time, Spurs' form dipped so badly that they were eventually relegated. As well as being a fine player, Rowe would have an even more important role to play at the club in years to come. Full-back Bill Whatley was another player to come through the ranks to emerge as a regular, while local product Johnny Morrison had joined Spurs in 1933 and it was Tresadern that gave the centre forward his chance in the side a few years later. Quick, brave and with a genuine striker's eye for goal, Morrison was a rare bright spot in the generally disappointing 1930s era at the club, playing so well he eventually made another fan-favourite, George Hunt, expendable. Hunt would later sign for Arsenal, incurring the wrath of all Spurs fans, whose distaste for their local rivals was growing all the time.

Among Tresadern's signings, those that proved best were Ralph Ward – a hard-nosed full-back – the diminutive Joe Meek and left-winger Les Miller, captured from French League side Sochaux. None of the signings were particularly glamorous and, although Ward was solid and reliable, both Meek and Miller had as many nondescript games as they did positive ones, the pair eventually floating into mediocrity.

With league form average at best, the FA Cup again provided a tonic in the 1936/37 season. The third round had incredibly seen Spurs beat high-flying First Division side Portsmouth 5–0 away, before ousting Plymouth 1–0 in round four. The fifth round pitched Spurs against one of the most exciting clubs of the era, Everton. In their ranks, Everton could boast two of the finest talents of the century, Dixie Dean and Tommy Lawton. Dean would become Everton's finest son, scoring an astonishing 473 goals in his career with the Merseyside club, while the blossoming talent that was the forward Lawton had already seen the youngster score a hat-trick on his debut at

Tottenham Hotspur 4	Everton 3
Morrison (3),	Lawton,
Meek	Dean (2)

Arthur Rowe in action.

just sixteen and – still only seventeen at the time of the match with Spurs – Lawton would develop into a high-class England international.

With 47,000 people wedged into a deeply excited White Hart Lane to watch the replay of the tie, the morning rain that had threatened to ruin proceedings wound up doing little to dampen spirits during this fantastic game. The groundsmen had toiled all morning to get the pitch in to a playable state and it was Everton that came out with all guns blazing. Young Lawton fired the visitors ahead after just two minutes and then, on twenty minutes, it was Geldrad – who had supplied Lawton with the cross for the opener – who was again the provider, this time Dean heading in from close range to put the visitors 2–0 up. Morrison was able to pull one back before half-time to give Spurs hope, but that hope was tested to the limit in the second half when the referee strangely disallowed a pair of Spurs goals, with no apparent explanation. It seemed that the gods were transpiring against Tottenham and, after having their opponents on the ropes they were caught out by a fast-paced Everton breakaway that finished with Lawton setting up Dean for a 3–1 lead.

As if seeking justice for the two disallowed goals, Spurs came forward again with even more intent. They first survived Everton being awarded a penalty when a foul-throw was spotted moments earlier, and soon after, the busy Morrison got his second of the day in the sixty-fifth minute, bringing the crowd to life. Then, just as all looked lost, Spurs staged a miracle finale. Thrusting forward with wave after wave of attack, the crowd erupted when Meek grabbed an equaliser on eighty-five minutes and were sent into an absolute frenzy when Morrison completed his hat-trick at the death, capping a most memorable Spurs comeback, and sending them through to the quarter-finals. The FA Cup dream was to end there however, as Spurs were beaten 3–1 at home by Preston North End.

A year later, with Tottenham again unable to gain promotion, the manager resigned, possibly fearing the sack, and he joined Plymouth. Given a hero's welcome, Peter McWilliam returned for a second spell in charge, but he failed to make any significant strides with the team and, when the Football League broke up again at the end of the 1939/40 season because of the outbreak of the Second World War, McWilliam decided he was too old to carry on with the job when the league resumed in 1946/47.

Tottenham Hotspur: J. Hall, Ward, Whatley, Buckingham, Rowe, Grice, McCormick, Meek, Morrison, Duncan, Miller

Everton: Sagar, Cook, Jones, Britton, Gee, Mercer, Geldard, Cunliffe, Dean, Lawton, Gillick

TOTTENHAM HOTSPUR v. NEWCASTLE UNITED

Date: 18 November 1950

Location: White Hart Lane

Match title: Football League First Division

Attendance: 70,336

After the Football League reconvened in 1946 following the Second World War, Spurs laboured in the Second Division for three years under the management of Joe Hulme. They were not a bad side in the late 1940s; it was just that they lacked that extra impetus to take them a step further. Little did the team know that, when new manager Arthur Rowe joined the club for the start of the 1949/50 season (replacing the sacked Hulme), it was not only a new boss they were getting, but also an imminent change in their style of play. Rowe had been an exceptional, footballing centre half for the club in the 1930s and had then delved into management, turning Chelmsford City into a thoroughly entertaining, pleasing-on-the-eye non-league side. Rowe's connections with Tottenham were not merely restricted to representation as a player, for he had been born in the vicinity of White Hart Lane and had watched in adulation as a supporter when Spurs won the FA Cup in 1921.

While already established as a team renowned for attacking play, flair and skill, it was Rowe's idea to change their actual style of play, while incorporating the traits with which the club had grown. His emphasis was passing and moving, or 'push and run' as it became known. Rowe believed in keeping possession away from the opposition through a combination of accurate passing and lightning-quick movement off the ball into space – 'simple and quick', as Rowe termed it. He also encouraged Spurs to attack as an entire team, and defend likewise. In the Second Division, Rowe's vision worked with resounding success. Spurs blitzed the division with their fast, and at times, breathtaking style. Their collective talents scored 81 league goals and yielded just 35 as the Second Division title was wrapped up long before the final game, and Spurs at last had won promotion.

Adamant in his beliefs about the way the game should be played, Rowe fully intended on continuing with 'push and run' in the top flight and, after an initial slow start, Spurs adapted to the superior demands and faster pace of the First Division and soon had teams sitting up and taking notice of their tantalising brand of football. In goal was the inspirational Ted Ditchburn, a son of a professional boxer and a 'keeper with such immense presence and bravery that he is rightfully considered – together with Pat Jennings – as Tottenham's greatest ever keeper, racking up 452 appearances for the club and winning 6 England caps. Manning the full-back positions were the reliable Arthur Willis and the cultured, fine-passing Alf Ramsey – a Rowe signing from Southampton – and a player seen as a key addition to the new-look Spurs. Of course, Ramsey would go on to great success in management, steering England to an unforgettable triumph in the 1966 World Cup. Signed by Hulme from lower league side Lovell's Athletic, Harry Clarke provided the perfect middle-man between Willis and Ramsey; his big, powerful frame ideally suited to the centre half spot. Another man with a serious future in football management – with Spurs – was Bill Nicholson, a player who had come up through the ranks to start at half-back with fine effect, and a player– like Ramsey – who fitted perfectly with Rowe's style, as did his half-back partner Ron Burgess, another great in Spurs' history who made his debut in 1938 and – excluding the war years – played 328 games for the club. Burgess was the captain, a player who exemplified everything that Rowe wanted from his team; intelligent, quick, strong if need be, and above all, supportive in both defence and attack. The wingers were fast, skilful and very much adaptable to 'push and run', with Sonny Walters on the right and Les Medley on

Tottenham Hotspur 7	Newcastle United 0
Bennett, Baily, Medley (3), Walters, Ramsey (pen.)	

Tottenham Hotspur v. Newcastle United

Eddie Baily.

the left. Les Bennett – an attacking midfielder – and the genial Eddie Baily manned the inside forward roles, with the fine all-round ability of Len Duquemin – born in the Channel Islands – spearheading the attack.

The first serious realisation that Spurs were becoming a force to be reckoned with arrived in November 1950 when Newcastle United, the recognised powerhouse of the division and reigning league champions, ventured to White Hart Lane for a hotly anticipated league encounter. There was no doubting Newcastle were a fine side, tough and strong, and possessed one of the finest marksmen in their history in the legendary Jackie Milburn.

What Spurs did to Newcastle that day sent shockwaves ringing through the division, as a new kid on the block emphatically announced itself. Over 70,000 somehow squeezed into White Hart Lane, with countless others unluckily stuck outside the ground unable to get in, and it was not long before the vast majority exploded into raptures as Baily's pinpoint cross was swept in by Bennett. Baily – who was having one of the many superb matches he enjoyed throughout the 1950/51 season – gave the crowd even more to cheer about after twenty-five minutes, robbing another of Newcastle's big stars, Joe Harvey, and darting in on goal before calmly placing the ball past the United 'keeper Fairbrother. The visitors appeared shocked, but Spurs were going for the jugular; their passing and general movement seemingly exhausting Newcastle. Medley struck twice in two minutes and Spurs went in at half time astonishingly 4–0 up against the champions.

Even though the captain Burgess was missing – his place taken by the capable Colin Brittan – Spurs refused to relent. The second half was nothing short of total domination. The Tottenham passing constantly cut Newcastle open and despite the visitors being reduced in number by one when McMichael left the game injured, it was a strange and almost eerie second half, as Spurs seemed to be playing on a different level against a very, very good team. Sonny Walters struck from twenty-five yards out, Medley completed his hat-trick, and the outstanding Ramsey stroked home a last-minute penalty to complete the destruction.

A 7–0 scoreline against the champions not only injected an immense portion of confidence and belief into Rowe's blossoming side, it also proved to the rest of the league that 'push and run' was not to be taken lightly and that Spurs were indeed, serious title contenders.

Tottenham Hotspur: Ditchburn, Ramsey, Willis, Nicholson, Clarke, Brittan, Walters, Bennett, Duquemin, Baily, Medley

Newcastle United: Unknown

TOTTENHAM HOTSPUR v. SHEFFIELD WEDNESDAY

Date: 28 April 1951

Location: White Hart Lane

Match title: Football League First Division

Attendance: 46,645

Having been given a rude awakening by Blackpool on their return to the First Division (a 4–1 reversal), there were some who doubted whether Arthur Rowe's 'push and run' philosophy could be a success in the top flight. However, Spurs gradually gained a foothold in the division and it was not long before their unique style – adapted to produce football at a swifter, more dynamic pace so as to counter for the stronger First Division teams – began to click. The 7–0 annihilation of champions Newcastle United in November was the highlight of a fantastic, eight-game winning streak that had begun in late September. Spurs were starting to score freely as their style swept aside some of the league's best defences. Indeed, in that eight-game streak, Spurs scored no fewer than 28 goals with just 6 conceded, showing that the side's total team-orientated attitude to defending and attacking was prospering. The winning run catapulted Spurs – who had started the season modestly – into second place in the table, with Arsenal leading the way, and the main title challengers at that stage appeared to be the two north London clubs, Manchester United, free-scoring Blackpool and the reigning champions Newcastle United. Although the winning streak was stopped with a 3–2 defeat at Huddersfield Town, Spurs continued to flourish, beating their big rivals Arsenal 1–0 at White Hart Lane two days before Christmas with a goal from the hugely influential Eddie Baily, having gained revenge on Blackpool a week earlier. The home form was outstanding, with results including a Len Duquemin-hat-trick-inspired 5–0 win against West Bromwich Albion in March, and the fact that Spurs failed to win only four of twenty-one league games at White Hart Lane put Tottenham in pole-position in the title race heading into the last few weeks of the season.

Infuriatingly, Huddersfield Town left White Hart Lane with a totally unexpected 2–0 in mid-April to give Tottenham's nearest league rivals Manchester United a glimmer of hope. When Spurs could only get a draw at Middlesbrough a week later, it was back to White Hart Lane for a nerve-racking encounter with Sheffield Wednesday. A win, and Spurs would be league champions for the first time in their history.

One of the secrets to Tottenham's success throughout the season was their good fortune in avoiding serious injuries, allowing them frequently to field a settled, balanced side. For the match with Sheffield Wednesday, this factor held true, with Spurs able to name their strongest eleven. The one position open to argument was inside right, where the tall, long-striding Len Bennett and Peter Murphy, a magnificent runner with the ball, had both featured regularly with success during the season. On this occasion, it was to be Murphy who was given the chance to shine.

Sheffield Wednesday had accompanied Spurs in promotion from the Second Division but, in stark contrast to Spurs, the Yorkshire club had struggled mightily at the highest level and, with a sieve-like defence, were involved in a dogfight for their First Division lives together with Huddersfield Town, Chelsea and Everton – two of whom faced relegation. It was this factor that guaranteed Wednesday would make life as difficult as possible for title-chasing Spurs, with the idea of simply gifting the championship to the north London club non-existent. As it turned out, the game was an extremely tight affair, Wednesday's defenders doing their utmost to destroy and deny Tottenham's fast-flowing football. But as awkward as the opposition were to play against on this particular occasion, Spurs had

---

Tottenham Hotspur 1

Duquemin

Sheffield Wednesday 0

Tottenham Hotspur v. Sheffield Wednesday

Len Duquemin got the goal that clinched the league title.

not reached where they were by playing bad football. All season long Spurs had proved infuriating and frustrating to compete with; their players always moving, interchanging positions and passing the ball about at pace and, just a minute before half-time, style was to overcome stubbornness when Duquemin poached the goal that sent the crowd wild. With just forty-five minutes to play, the title was now very much in Tottenham's grasp.

There was tension and excitement among the large crowd as the realisation grew that Spurs were on the threshold of something huge. Spurs came forward in the second half – albeit in a less adventurous manner than usual – but they could not find a second, decisive goal. It was up to Wednesday to force the issue but, with Ditchburn aggressively marshalling his defence and Ramsey, Nicholson and Burgess calmly asserting their authority, the visitors could find no way through. Duquemin's goal had been enough to win the league for Spurs, and their fans were ecstatic at the final whistle.

Spurs had taken the league by storm with their 'push and run' game, exciting fans of all clubs up and down the country with their play. At times, they had been prolific, scoring a league-leading 82 goals, for which the main contributors were Sonny Walters (15), Len Duquemin (14), Eddie Baily (11), Les Medley (11), Peter Murphy (9) and Len Bennett (7). The defence had been solid too, with the intelligent and quick-thinking Alf Ramsey and Bill Nicholson, the experienced captain Ron Burgess and of course the great Ted Ditchburn in goal. The secret was that they all played as a team, each man fitting like pieces of a jigsaw into the master scheme, as if they had been born to play in the desired style. By common consensus, the real star was inside left Eddie Baily, a wonderful, natural footballer. Baily had broken into the Spurs side in 1947 and when Rowe began to introduce 'push and run', it was Baily who was perhaps the finest exponent of the style. An accurate passer with a exquisite first touch, Baily simply excelled in the scheme, using his abundant skills to set up chances for others as well as being able to glide into goal-scoring positions where he was able to maximise his silver-bullet shooting. Later on, when Nicholson himself became manager, Baily stayed on at Spurs as assistant coach, playing his part behind the scenes in another great Spurs side.

Masterminding the whole success was Arthur Rowe. A high-quality player, Rowe had risen to new heights as manager taking, in the space of two years, a big club floundering in the Second Division to the First Division championship, playing in a style very much of his own creation and lending strong argument for the right for his Spurs side to be labelled the best ever at Tottenham Hotspur Football Club.

Tottenham Hotspur: Ditchburn, Ramsey, Willis, Nicholson, Clarke, Burgess, Walters, Murphy, Duquemin, Baily, Medley

Sheffield Wednesday: Unknown

TOTTENHAM HOTSPUR v. EVERTON

Date: 11 October 1958

Location: White Hart Lane

Match title: Football League First Division

Attendance: 37,794

Following their rapid rise from the Second Division to champions of the First, many assumed Spurs would remain locked at the peak of English football for a number of years to come. Quite simply, it was never going to be so straightforward, and Arthur Rowe was aware of this. In just two years he had built his 'push and run' side and made it the most breathtaking, mesmerising team in the land. However, just as quickly as that team had risen to prominence, opponents latched on to ways to disrupt – and at times – totally destroy the free-flowing Tottenham style. Even so, Spurs still managed to finish second in 1951/52, but were out-pointed by Manchester United for the title. Another problem emerging steadily was that a number of the key members of the team from the previous few years – such as Bill Nicholson, Ron Burgess and Eddie Baily – were beginning to slow down, and Rowe knew the time was not far off when he would have to blood new, younger players. By the end of the 1952/53 season, opponents had worked out how best to thwart 'push and run', using tight, stifling marking. With the team no longer the force of old, Spurs could only manage tenth place in the league behind rivals Arsenal and slumped to a disturbing position of sixteenth the following season behind champions Wolves.

The Arthur Rowe era came to an unhappy end at the conclusion of the 1954/55 season when the manager of one of the all-time great Tottenham sides resigned because of poor health. However, Rowe left Tottenham having pulled one final masterstroke, a piece of business that cements his status as one of the club's finest managers. Paying £30,000 and outbidding Arsenal in the process, Rowe secured the services of the mercurial Danny Blanchflower from Aston Villa. It was Rowe's assistant Jimmy Anderson who took over and, although he struggled in his first season in charge (Spurs finished eighteenth), he was certainly laying the foundations for a side that had the potential to push for honours. In a pressurised three and a half years in charge, Anderson was able to blood promising home-grown talent in defenders Peter Baker and Ron Henry as well as the little Yorkshire-born winger Terry Dyson, sign excellent forwards Bobby Smith and Terry Medwin, giant centre half Maurice Norman and, later, dynamic Welsh winger Cliff Jones, as well as helping to phase Blanchflower into the team. It was also Anderson who gave the reigns to the much-blessed talent and skill of the fly-like Tommy Harmer to impact the side. The tiny, lightweight Harmer had joined the club in 1948 but, owing principally to fears about his diminutive size, it was not until Anderson became manager that this little player with a razor-like mind and wonderful skills was allowed to feature regularly.

The signs were good that Anderson was building another useful Spurs team. They finished runners-up in the First Division (again to Manchester United) in 1956/57 and came third behind the best side of the mid to late 1950s, Wolves, a year later. But against expectation, the results at the start of the 1958/59 season were terrible and Anderson – always in the shadow of his predecessor's glories – began to feel the heat, and a few months into the season, he resigned. Taking his place was a man so pivotal in Rowe's great team – Bill Nicholson. In truth, Nicholson became manager of Spurs at just the right time. Already adored by the home fans, Nicholson succeeded a man in Anderson who, although fairly successful, had failed to deliver a trophy to White Hart Lane and who had left the new boss with a most promising squad of players that, with one or two additions, had the

Tottenham Hotspur 10

Smith (4), Stokes (2), Robb, Medwin, Harmer, Ryden

Everton 4

J. Harris (3), Collins

34

TOTTENHAM HOTSPUR v. EVERTON

*Bobby Smith heads Spurs'
seventh goal past Everton
goalkeeper Albert Dunlop.*

potential to disrupt the hierarchy of the First Division, namely Wolves and Manchester United. Nicholson's first game was at home to Everton, and the outcome of the game would prove to be as emphatic and stunning as Nicholson's career as manager of Spurs.

As if rising to a new manager's expectations, it was a day when some of the finest names in the history of Tottenham Hotspur – Blanchflower, Harmer, Medwin and Smith – were truly outstanding. There were just three minutes on the clock when forward Alfie Stokes put Spurs in front and, incredibly, it would be the first of seven first-half goals – six of which would belong to Spurs. Everton were level on ten minutes when Jimmy Harris scored, but Spurs went right down the other end following the restart and a pinpoint cross was met with bullet-like power from the head of the tall, robust centre forward, Bobby Smith. Blanchflower split the Everton defence with an arrow-like pass that sent the swift George Robb through on goal, and the winger fired past the Everton goalkeeper Dunlop, giving Spurs a 3–1 lead. Terry Medwin had been causing all sorts of problems for the Everton defence on the right wing and, moments before half-time, he struck for a sixth Spurs goal, with both Stokes and Smith having scored their second goals of the game prior to that. With tremendous appreciation from the crowd, Spurs went in at half-time 6–1 ahead.

In an era of attack-minded teams, Everton's defence was more susceptible than most to conceding goals, yet Tottenham's – at the time – was equally porous, and it was no surprise when the hard-working Everton front line forced a second goal at the start of the second half, again courtesy of Harris. But Harmer and Blanchflower were truly dictating proceedings with their passing and clever thinking, threatening to carve open the visitors at every opportunity, and so it proved, with the latter epitomising his play not only on the day but throughout his Spurs career by bringing the ball out of the Tottenham half and setting Smith clear to bulldoze to his hat-trick, while Harmer brought rich applause (he was a definite fan favourite) from the crowd when he cracked home an eighth for Spurs ten minutes from time. The final few minutes were wild and crazy, with both sides swapping goals like Christmas presents; Harris once more for Everton, Smith again for Spurs, Collins for the visitors before centre half John Ryden nudged home Tottenham's tenth and final goal in a pulsating, almost surreal game.

By winning 10–4, Spurs had recorded their most emphatic triumph since thrashing a high-class Newcastle United side 7–0 in the 1950/51 championship season. Even though no honours awaited them in this particular campaign – they would finish eighteenth in the league – the seeds were being sown for future success, and the glory, glory days were not far away from returning to White Hart Lane.

Tottenham Hotspur: Hollowbread, Baker, Hopkins, Blanchflower, Ryden, Hey, Medwin, Harmer, Smith, Stokes, Robb

Everton: Dunlop, Sanders, Branwell, King, Jones, B. Harris, Fielding, J. Harris, Hickson, Collins, O'Hara

Tottenham Hotspur v. Crewe Alexandra

Date: 3 February 1960

Location: White Hart Lane

Match title: FA Cup fourth round replay

Attendance: 64,365

There was no doubt that Bill Nicholson had inherited the basis of a very good side from his predecessor Jimmy Anderson but, as illustrated by the club's final league position in 1958/59, there remained much to improve upon. Nicholson realised the team needed more steel in the defence and half-back line, as well as an extra dose of guile and general class among the forwards.

At the back end of the previous season, Nicholson made his first and perhaps most influential signing during his time in charge of Spurs. He signed fiery Scot Dave Mackay from Hearts. Mackay would go on to enjoy a dominant career in the Spurs midfield, becoming one of the finest players of his era and establishing himself as a true Spurs legend. Also joining the club before the end of 1959 were Bill Brown, a solid, reliable goalkeeper and the best Spurs had had at the position since the heyday of Ted Ditchburn; natural goalscorer Les Allen (not the last of his namesake to wear the white shirt of Tottenham), and the brilliant, graceful attacking talent of another Scot, John White, who signed from Falkirk and was, by common consensus, the final piece in Nicholson's Spurs jigsaw.

The 1959/60 campaign – Nicholson's first full season in charge – began in highly promising fashion as the team went twelve games unbeaten. By the end of March, they sat proudly at the top of the division, beginning to play the fast-tempo style of football that had made the club famous, but with perhaps a touch more versatility to their game than previous Spurs sides. They had physical players in giant centre half Maurice Norman, burly centre forward Bobby Smith and of course Mackay and, while the team's style was again based primarily on a sound passing game, they also developed a tough, battling edge to their play that would help them progress in to becoming the team of the 1960s.

They also possessed natural leaders in Mackay and the super-intelligent and highly talented Danny Blanchflower, the man who was at the heart of all that was good about Bill Nicholson's Tottenham Hotspur.

Spurs were fast becoming not only an entertaining side but one that was developing into a powerful, title-challenging unit, yet the 1959/60 season was just that little bit too early for them to capture the league crown. Wolves had been the most superior side of the second half of the 1950s, but they were to be denied a third consecutive title by Burnley, who took the First Division championship by a mere point. Like Spurs, Burnley would feature as one of the best sides of the 1960s.

Spurs had bravely finished just two points (five home defeats proving their ultimate downfall) behind champions Burnley and a point behind runners-up Wolves, showing they were a team on the verge of breaking through in the league, yet it was a result in the FA Cup that proved to be the highlight of the season.

The fourth round of the FA Cup had pitched Spurs against Crewe Alexandra of the Third Division and there were few outside of Crewe who anticipated anything other than a Spurs win when the two teams met at Gresty Road. However, Crewe displayed unflinching courage and grit, and in the end, Spurs were given the fright of their lives as the game ended 2–2.

In the three days between the first match and the replay, Tottenham came in for a barrage of criticism over their performance at Crewe. However, as if awoken like a sleeping tiger, Spurs would make no mistake at White Hart Lane.

Tottenham Hotspur 13

Allen (5), Smith (3),
Jones (3, 1 pen.), Harmer (2)

Crewe Alexandra 2

Coleman,
Llewellyn

TOTTENHAM HOTSPUR v. CREWE ALEXANDRA

Les Allen scored five goals for Spurs against Crewe.

In surely the most incredible first half in the club's history, the enormous crowd at White Hart Lane were treated to eleven goals – ten by the home side. Les Allen got four, Bobby Smith three, Tommy Harmer two and the inspirational Welsh right-winger, Cliff Jones, one. Somewhere in the minefield that was becoming the Crewe goalmouth, the visitors had managed to gain possession of the ball long enough to mount an attack of their own and scored a goal themselves, through Coleman and, to their credit, the Third Division side never gave in, although obviously the score depicted a mismatch.

Jones grabbed another at the start of the second half, then for half an hour the scoring relented as both players and fans alike appeared to pause to catch their breath. Spurs struck a twelfth when the razor-sharp Allen pounced to net his fifth before Llewellyn brought some joy to the beleaguered travelling fans by striking his side's second. Cliff Jones, arguably the best winger in the club's history, rounded off the scoring late on when slotting home a penalty after he himself had been brought down.

Spurs did not win the FA Cup in the 1959/60 season, but the result stands out in their history as being their biggest win ever.

Tottenham Hotspur: Brown, Hills, Henry, Blanchflower, Norman, Mackay, White, Harmer, Smith, Allen, Jones

Crewe Alexandra: Evans, Millar, Campbell, D. Jones, Willmott, Warhurst, Coleman, Riley, Llewellyn, Keery, M. Jones

TOTTENHAM HOTSPUR v. SHEFFIELD WEDNESDAY

Date: 17 April 1961

Location: White Hart Lane

Match title: Football League First Division

Attendance: 61,205

The start of the 1960/61 season could not have gone any better for Tottenham Hotspur. Building on the promise they had shown the season before, Spurs began the season with all guns blazing, literally taking the division by storm. Of the opening sixteen games stretching to the middle of November, Spurs sensationally won fifteen, drawing the other and scoring an incredible 53 goals in the process – centre forward Bobby Smith in particularly fine form during the span, netting 15 times. Some of the division's best sides, such as Everton, Manchester United, Arsenal, Aston Villa and Wolves, were beaten during the run and not only were they beaten but they were beaten handsomely, with Spurs again delighting their supporters – as well, by and large, those of their rivals – with a splendid, neat, quick passing and a thoroughly effective style of play, at times simply outclassing their opposition. It was a start of unrivalled brilliance, and served notice that this truly was a special team that Bill Nicholson had put together, a fact that was duly accepted in time.

By the time Spurs played at Sheffield Wednesday in November, it was generally considered that this 'Super Spurs' team were now favourites for the title. Sheffield Wednesday however, were also a team on the rise and had started the new campaign well, having finished fifth the season before. It was the Yorkshire club that had run out winners in the season's first league meeting between the two, Wednesday winning the match 2–1 and thus inflicting the season's first league defeat on Spurs and bringing to an end their wonderful unbeaten run. The win for Sheffield Wednesday gave them hope of overhauling the Londoners in the long run, but Spurs were to respond by taking their game to another level, not losing again until a 2–0 reversal at Manchester United in mid-January, and again scoring goals at will. Once the FA Cup campaign began in January, the Spurs steam train that was threatening to run away with the First Division was slowed somewhat, with a stretch of lower-scoring draws and defeats, but the cup run swept Spurs all the way to the final and, with that match coming after the league season was over, Spurs could concentrate all their efforts on the last batch of league games. A four-game winning streak beginning at the end of March set up a rematch with Sheffield Wednesday at White Hart Lane; a win would guarantee the title. The game was played on a Monday night before an enormous crowd at White Hart Lane, and there was a mixture of both excitement and tremendous tension, an atmosphere that was reflected in the match itself.

Throughout the season, Spurs had played with a panache and authority that led many to believe this particular side to be the finest league team of all time – Tottenham or any other club. However, the game against Sheffield Wednesday was a far different occasion, with the result the be all and end all, nerves understandably playing a huge part in proceedings. Spurs saw a lot of the ball early on, Blanchflower and Mackay prompting the attacks, yet there seemed a lack of willingness to commit to the sort of football they knew best, and the opening exchanges were certainly cluttered with caution. Perhaps they needed to be shocked into life. The crowd were definitely shocked when Sheffield Wednesday were awarded a free-kick after an innocuous-looking challenge involving Maurice Norman and the visitors' centre forward John Fantham. From the resulting kick, Don Megson blasted his shot straight into the Spurs wall, but when the ball bounced back into his path, Megson was given

Tottenham Hotspur 2	Sheffield Wednesday 1
Smith,	Megson
Allen	

TOTTENHAM HOTSPUR v. SHEFFIELD WEDNESDAY

The double-winning side of 1961. From left to right, back row: Brown, Baker, Henry, Blanchflower, Norman, Mackay, Nicholson. Front row: Jones, White, Smith, Allen, Dyson.

a second chance, and with that attempt he was able to fire his shot past Bill Brown in the Spurs goal. Megson's goal was greeted with ghost-like silence from the Spurs faithful, but it was not long before their team had them in full voice again. The opening goal served as a reminder to Spurs as to what was at stake, and they seemed more determined not to let their chance go to waste.

Although Spurs were beginning to play some decent football, Wednesday's rearguard was holding firm, until a moment of brilliance lifted the tension in the ground with three minutes remaining before half-time. A long clearance out of defence by full-back Peter Baker was glanced on by the smallest player in the Spurs team, winger Terry Dyson. The flick went from the smallest player to the most robust, Bobby Smith, and almost in a role-reversal with Dyson, it was Smith who showed exceptional skill to lift the ball over an on-rushing Wednesday defender before cracking a fierce shot past goalkeeper Ron Springett. The crowd went wild as the pressure in the ground was deflated almost instantly. For Spurs, the game was now there for the taking, and no sooner had Wednesday kicked off again than the visitors had conceded a needless free-kick. Floating a ball into the box, Danny Blanchflower's kick was knocked on by Norman to Les Allen, who drilled home and sent Spurs into the interval with a 2–1 lead.

The second half was filled once more with tension, some serious defending and no small amount of clock-watching by the home fans, but when the referee Tommy Dawes eventually blew the final whistle, Spurs players threw their arms up in joy amid realisation of what they had achieved. The margin by which Spurs won the title was eight points, with Sheffield Wednesday runners-up, and rarely has a league champion been so dominant throughout a campaign. Spurs scored an unbelievable 115 league goals in 1960/61 with the leading marksmen being Bobby Smith with 28, Les Allen (23), Cliff Jones (15), John White (13) and Terry Dyson (12).

Amid all the jubilation of their second league championship, Spurs knew their season was not yet complete. Their fine FA Cup run had taken Spurs all the way to the final and a date with Leicester City. The final would be Tottenham's first ever at Wembley Stadium. Win there, and a groundbreaking league and cup double would be theirs.

Tottenham Hotspur: Brown, Baker, Henry, Blanchflower, Norman, Mackay, Jones, White, Smith, Allen, Dyson

Sheffield Wednesday: Unknown

Tottenham Hotspur v. Leicester City

Date: 6 May 1961

Location: Wembley Stadium

Match title: FA Cup final

Attendance: 100,000

Tottenham had indeed been mightily impressive when winning the First Division championship. Nicholson had opted for players who possessed excellent control and, like Arthur Rowe before him, he preached movement off the ball and swift, accurate passing. Although not as lightning-quick in their running as Rowe's team, this Spurs side was every bit as slick and, in all probability, more effective, for they had different weapons in their game, offering versatility, and for that, they won an unfathomable number of admirers – not just from north London.

Spurs had readily swept the First Division playing Nicholson's way and when Danny Blanchflower accepted the league trophy in the company of his teammates in the stands at White Hart Lane at the conclusion of the final league game against West Bromwich Albion, those present in the ground knew they had witnessed a team worthy of being considered as the best club side of the century. But Spurs had one more fixture to play before the season was over: the small matter of the FA Cup final at Wembley. If they could overcome Leicester City (who had finished sixth in the First Division) then Spurs could truly be labelled a great side, for no team in the twentieth century had completed the league and cup double, although a number had gone close, including the two best sides of the 1950s, Wolves and Manchester United. The game was an opportunity for Spurs to boldly carve their name in history, ensuring this particular team and their enchanting style of play would never be forgotten.

The cup run had begun in January with an exciting 3–2 victory at home to Charlton before Spurs were paired with Crewe Alexandra for the second year running in the fourth round. Crewe had given Spurs all sorts of problems in the first encounter the season before (although Spurs incredibly won the replay 13–2 having drawn 2–2 at Gresty Road), but on this occasion the First Division side rolled to a comfortable 5–1 victory. Aston Villa were Tottenham's fifth round opponents and, having already beaten the Midlands club 6–2 and 2–1 in the league (the latter result coming just a week before the teams met in the FA Cup), Spurs were heavily fancied and, on the day, were never troubled, winning 2–0 at Villa Park. Second Division Sunderland, however, provided a far sterner test in the quarter-final, offering Spurs as physical a match-up as they had faced all season, and in the first game at Roker Park, Spurs were thankful that a Cliff Jones goal gave them an opportunity for a replay at White Hart Lane four days later. In front of their own fans, Spurs found the going much easier, running out 5–0 winners and setting up a semi-final clash with Burnley, which would be played at the neutral venue of Villa Park. The match was billed as the defending league champions (Burnley) against the new champions and was one of the most highly anticipated games in years. In their league meeting at White Hart Lane in early December, Spurs had led 4–0 at one point before Burnley had stormed back to earn a 4–4 draw. In the semi-final, however, the new superstars outclassed the old guard, Spurs achieving a surprisingly easy 3–0 win, with Jones and Bobby Smith (2) scoring the goals that took Spurs to Wembley for the first time. In the other semi-final, Leicester emerged from a three-game marathon with Sheffield United, eventually winning in a second replay.

Spurs had enjoyed a remarkably injury free season and at Wembley they were able to field their strongest side, a side fully expected to take the cup back to White Hart Lane. In goal was Bill Brown, who had quietly become

---

Tottenham Hotspur 2

Smith,

Dyson

Leicester City 0

Tottenham Hotspur v. Leicester City

Bobby Smith (9) is on the ground but has just opened the scoring for Spurs.

Tottenham's safest keeper since the best days of Ted Ditchburn. Right-back was Peter Baker, a player who had come up through the ranks at Spurs and was quick-thinking and combative. At left-back was Ron Henry, a player who had broken into the team when Welshman Mel Hopkins had suffered an injury and had kept his place ever since. Henry was far from the most gifted player in the Spurs side, but he was a super tackler and was relentless in his defending, rarely caught out of position. The giant figure of Maurice Norman manned the centre half spot and, as one would expect, he won everything in the air. Norman could pass the ball too, and his height made him a dangerous weapon in the opposition penalty area from free-kicks and corners.

Then there were the half-backs; each was as vital as the other and were two of the finest names in the history of the club. It would be difficult to imagine the success of Nicholson's side being achieved without Danny Blanchflower or Dave Mackay. Suffice to say that they were both extremely special players; Blanchflower the thinker, with wonderful passing ability covering all ranges, a sabre-like brain and a voice of encouragement, organisation and leadership for his teammates. Mackay was the motor of the team, never shirked a challenge, had as much quality in defence as he did going forward, and had instilled within him the will to win of a born warrior. The right side of the attack was unquestionably the best in the land. Flying like a bird down the right wing was Welshman Cliff Jones, one of the finest wingers of his era and perhaps the best Spurs ever possessed

Tottenham Hotspur: Brown, Baker, Henry, Blanchflower, Norman, Mackay, Jones, White, Smith, Allen, Dyson

Leicester City: Banks, Chalmers, Norman, McLintock, King, Appleton, Riley, Walsh, McIlmoyle, Keyworth, Cheesebrough

Tottenham Hotspur v. Leicester City

Spurs parade the cup around the Wembley pitch.

in the position, his play creating countless opportunities, and he also scored more than his fair share of goals. At inside right was John White, nicknamed 'The Ghost' for his ability to drift past defenders with the grace and ease of an exceptional player. White too was an instigator for many Tottenham goals, and his link play and thought process in combination with Jones and Blanchflower was a key reason as to why Spurs were so effective.

Little Terry Dyson played on the left wing, although he was rivalled for a place in the team continuously by the right-footed Terry Medwin, yet Dyson was a perfect foil for the more gifted players in the team, possessing a willingness and work ethic that defenders found hard to match, as well as being the provider of many a fine cross and no small number of goals. Inside Dyson was the talented Les Allen, a man whose career took off when he joined Spurs from Chelsea, but a man who would be the one to suffer most from the imminent arrival of a certain Jimmy Greaves. Allen – like his son Clive in future years – was a fine goalscorer, although he also had a good all-round game that helped gel the side, and his contribution to the team during the season was priceless, registering 27 league and cup goals. Finally, there was Bobby Smith who was tall, as strong as an ox and, for a man his size, not short on skill. The goal he scored to clinch the title against Sheffield Wednesday had proved he was more than just a target man, although his physical presence certainly gave Spurs an added edge to their game.

As in that game with Wednesday, Spurs began the cup final somewhat slowly, although White missed a golden opportunity to put Spurs in front after just three minutes. As expected, Leicester fought hard to quash the superior skill and passing of Tottenham, and their defence – marshalled by the excellent Gordon Banks in goal – was proving an extremely tough nut to crack. However, City suffered a severe blow in the first half when their right-back Len Chalmers was injured following an ugly-looking foul by Les Allen. With no substitutes at that period in football, Chalmers was moved to a less exposed position on the left wing, but his movement was cruelly limited, thus virtually sentencing Leicester to play the rest of the game with ten men.

TOTTENHAM HOTSPUR *v.* LEICESTER CITY

Spurs were struggling to meet the standards they had set throughout the season, and their frustration grew when Jones had a goal disallowed on thirty-eight minutes. With neither side sparkling, the game got a jolt in the arm in the sixty-sixth minute when Smith scored a goal for Spurs every bit as vital and impressive as his goal against Sheffield Wednesday in the league. Dyson slid a pass in to Smith who, on the penalty-spot, had his back to goal. In the blink of an eye, Smith turned his defender and unleashed a low shot of raw power past Banks to give Spurs the lead. Then, nine minutes later, Smith crossed from the right and there was Dyson (who had squandered a similar chance earlier) to head home Tottenham's second and ignite the wild celebrations for the Spurs fans.

With Leicester now a broken team and unable to threaten Spurs, the champions cruised through the remainder of the game and ran out comfortable 2–0 winners, despite the fact Leicester had been somewhat unfortunate regarding the Chalmers injury. Manager Bill Nicholson received a great deal of credit, and rightly so. Having learned from Arthur Rowe, Nicholson had maintained many of his former manager's principles, as well as offering a few extra options. True, some of the team was in place when he joined, but it still remained for Nicholson to blend those players with his own signings such as Mackay, White and Allen.

The outcome was a striking success and Tottenham had become the first club since 1897 to win the double, and the team of 1960/61 will always be remembered as one of the great sides in English football history.

TOTTENHAM HOTSPUR v. GORNIK ZABRZE

Date: 20 September 1961

Location: White Hart Lane

Match title: European Cup prel. rd 2nd leg

Attendance: 56,737

Tottenham's magnificent achievement in the First Division had brought with it a new challenge for the famous club. As champions, they had earned the right to play in the European Cup, and so a new chapter was opened in the history of Spurs. Their first ever venture into European competition had pitted Spurs against the tough, European battled-hardened Polish champions, Gornik Zabrze, and the anticipation of Tottenham unleashing their distinctive brand of football on the finest clubs the Continent had to offer was a mouth-watering prospect.

If Spurs thought the Poles were going to succumb as easily as some of the sides in the First Division, they were in for a rude shock. Spurs travelled to a bleak, obscure Polish outpost for the first leg and were greeted by a baying rabble of over 70,000, roaring every positive action the Poles took – and they had much to roar about. After only eight minutes, Gornik took the lead, and when they sailed in to a 4–0 advantage early in the second half it appeared Tottenham's first taste of European football would be a bitter one. But late goals from Cliff Jones and Terry Dyson meant a 4–2 reversal, although somewhat unexpected, was not as bad as it could have been.

Nonetheless, Spurs had received a timely wake-up call in Poland, and it was obvious that, if they were to be successful in Europe, they were going to have to adapt and learn new ways of playing, especially away from home. It was up to Nicholson to get his players – well equipped in principle for the demands of European competition – moulded into the desired team if they were going to progress deep into the European Cup. In fairness to Tottenham, they had never played before in competitive European competition, and the first-leg result had left them partially stunned. They had been cavalier but naïve in Poland, outmanoeuvred tactically by a typical Eastern European outfit. In the return leg, however, things would be much different.

Fittingly, it was the usual team that had led Spurs to the double the season before that ran out for the first of many European nights at White Hart Lane, but it was now the Poles who were favourites to progress after what had happened in the first leg. Even so, a stupendously large and vocal crowd jammed in to White Hart Lane, and the atmosphere appeared to affect Gornik negatively as, straight from the start, Spurs charged forward as if to demonstrate to their opponents that this was the way they had intended to play in the first leg. From the moment Danny Blanchflower struck from an early penalty, the writing was on the wall for the Polish side, as Spurs attacked relentlessly like a pack of hungry dogs. Jones scored the second soon after, and Gornik – visibly wilting under the pressure – conceded three more before half-time, with the brilliant Jones striking his second of the game with a fierce left-footed blast, the Welshman also firing home Tottenham's fourth before Bobby Smith – a constant menace and physical hazard for the Polish defence – rammed in the fifth just prior to the break. During Tottenham's blitz-like start, Gornik had managed a goal of their own, but with Spurs now 7–5 ahead on aggregate and smelling blood, any chance of a Polish comeback was non-existent.

Not only does this match have obvious historical significance, being the first European night at the Lane, but it also goes down as one of the best performances in terms of character by this particular Tottenham team. The way they overcame a serious setback in Poland to regroup, adjust and ultimately destroy Gornik was highly admirable,

Tottenham Hotspur 8
Blanchflower (pen.), Jones (3),
Smith (2), Dyson, White

Gornik Zabrze 1
Pohl

Dyson watches in delight as Smith's (out of picture) header beats Gornik goalkeeper Kostka.

and proved to all that, if they could alter their tactics favourably away from home, Spurs were most definitely a match for any European side at White Hart Lane, where the support was guaranteed to be tremendous.

Second-half goals from Smith, Dyson and John White completed the 8–1 mauling, and Spurs were on the march in Europe.

Tottenham Hotspur: Brown, Baker, Henry, Blanchflower, Norman, Mackay, Jones, White, Smith, Allen, Dyson

Gornik Zabrze: Unknown

TOTTENHAM HOTSPUR v. BENFICA

Date: 5 April 1962   **Match title:** European Cup semi-final 2nd leg

Location: White Hart Lane   **Attendance:** 64,448

Having ultimately slain Gornik Zabrze in the preliminary round of the 1961/62 European Cup, Spurs next disposed of Feyenoord and Dukla Prague. The Dutch champions were beaten 4–2 on aggregate while, in the next round, an impressive 4–1 victory at White Hart Lane in the second leg saw Spurs through 4–2 over the two legs against the team from Czechoslovakia.

The most significant change at Tottenham since they started their European adventure had been the signing of forward Jimmy Greaves from AC Milan. Greaves, as natural, graceful and instinctive a goalscorer as one could wish to see, had started his career at Chelsea, swiftly developing into a striker of the highest order. When AC Milan had signed Greaves in 1961, the player had been sceptical of making the move and, after just four unsettled and largely unhappy months in Italy (although even in difficult circumstances he scored his fair share of goals), Bill Nicholson brought Greaves back to England, signing him for £99,999. Greaves is regarded as Tottenham's finest ever goalscorer and arguably the finest player ever to pull on the famous white shirt. Lightning-quick, intelligent and ruthless, Greaves was quite literally a footballing genius, a very special player indeed. In 379 games for Spurs, Greaves scored 266 goals. Jimmy Greaves' big-name signing only seemed to provide Spurs with more reason to believe that they could win the European Cup at the first time of asking. He scored a hat-trick on his league debut against Blackpool in December 1961, and by the time of the European Cup semi-final, he had already scored 18 times for Tottenham.

Spurs had been drawn to play the outstanding Portuguese champions Benfica in the semi-final, and faced a trip to the awesome Stadium of Light in the first leg. Benfica boasted some truly world-class players, including the uncompromising duo of Coluna and Germano, the fleet-footed winger Simoes, the inspirational captain and centre forward Aguas, and a man who would in time acquire legendary status and would star for Portugal in the 1966 World Cup, the 'Black Pearl', Eusebio, then just a youngster. Despite a noted penchant for skilful, attacking football, Benfica's tactics in the first leg left many – not least the Tottenham players – disillusioned and disappointed with this fine side. The Benfica players could have been mistaken for lumberjacks as they chopped and hacked at every one of the Spurs team throughout the ninety minutes. However, what really riled the Spurs players was the fact that referee Mr Poulsen, from Denmark, did nothing to punish the brutal tactics of the Portuguese, appearing oblivious to the harsh treatment Benfica were distributing. To make matters worse for Tottenham, Mr Poulsen disallowed two Spurs goals from Smith and Greaves with highly dubious offside decisions and, although Smith scored another goal that was allowed, Benfica struck three times to take a huge advantage to the match in north London, although they had made very few friends in doing so, which was sad because they possessed an abundance of talent and flair.

The second leg at White Hart Lane is recognised as one of the most exciting games of football ever played on the ground, and was a game piled with tension and drama. For Spurs, Nicholson had opted for a slightly defensive approach in Benfica but, in the second leg, he recalled the attacking right-winger Terry Medwin in place of the more defensive Tony Marchi, and what followed was a truly pulsating game of football, although this

Tottenham Hotspur 2	**Benfica 1**
Smith,	Aguas
Blanchflower (pen.)	

Tottenham Hotspur v. Benfica

Smith scores against Benfica.

too would be a match of high controversy. Flying out of the gates, as was their custom, Spurs tore at Benfica from the outset, hoping to create early opportunities so to put severe pressure on the Portuguese. But playing classic counterattack football with no small measure of skill, it was Benfica that rocked Tottenham and stunned the huge crowd of almost 65,000 when Aguas slid in an early goal with Bill Brown stranded. Momentarily shackled by the setback, Spurs proceeded to pummel the Benfica defence as if still in a rage over the controversy of the first leg. After twenty-four minutes, their efforts seemed rewarded when John White crossed to Smith, who then turned the ball on to Greaves who clinically dispatched what he believed was his first European goal for Spurs. Peeling away in delight to celebrate, Greaves turned in disbelief to see the Benfica players hassling the referee. The reason for this was that the linesman had flagged for offside, and again it was a mystery as to why. Three goals disallowed in mysterious circumstances during a major semi-final would have destroyed the spirit of most teams, but this was a very special Spurs side and forward they came again. Finally, on thirty-eight minutes, White – having one of the most influential games of his Tottenham career – curved a wicked ball into the Benfica box, which was controlled instantly by Smith and driven with venom into the net.

There was now fresh hope and, willed on by the frenetic crowd, Spurs began the second half in the same charging style. Barely four minutes had elapsed since the interval when White played a one-two with Smith and penetrated the Benfica penalty area before being tripped by the defender Cruz, and Spurs were awarded a penalty. Under what must have been the most unbearable pressure, Blanchflower coolly kept his nerve, raising the roof as his kick hit the net. Incredibly, Spurs now had every chance of overhauling Benfica. But as much as Spurs attacked – and they attacked with considerable urgency – the elusive third goal would not come. They should have had another penalty when Medwin's shot was handled by Germano but no decision was given, and Spurs knew the luck was not with them when a shot by Mackay hit the bar and bounced to safety.

So it was Benfica that progressed, 4-3 on aggregate, and went on to beat Real Madrid in the final. For Spurs, the result had been heart-breaking. They had given their all and been cruelly denied, and not only by Benfica. It had been an enthralling match, however, and served as a real introduction of Spurs to Europe, and the impression they made was most favourable. It had been a thoroughly exciting night, yet sadly not a glory, glory night – those days would come, however.

Tottenham Hotspur: Brown, Baker, Henry, Blanchflower, Norman, Mackay, Medwin, White, Smith, Greaves, Jones

Benfica: Unknown

TOTTENHAM HOTSPUR v. BURNLEY

Date: 5 May 1962   **Match title:** FA Cup final

Location: Wembley Stadium   **Attendance:** 100,000

The 1961/62 season was one of the most eventful and memorable in the history of Tottenham Hotspur Football Club. They had embarked on their first ever European campaign, signed a player in Jimmy Greaves who would become their all-time leading goalscorer, and had made a bold run at defending their league title from the previous season. Tottenham's league form – particularly at the beginning of the season – was far more patchy than in the previous campaign and, of the first nine fixtures, three games were lost and another two drawn, all a far cry from their supersonic start to the 'double' season. However, as the winter months arrived, so too did Greaves, and with him, Spurs seemed to change into a different gear. Ten victories were notched between the end of September and the turn of the year and, despite some inexplicable reversals in the second half of the season, Spurs stayed in the thick of the title hunt with Burnley as the league campaign reached its climax. But perhaps the most damaging league defeat came in the middle of March when Ipswich Town visited White Hart Lane. Managed by former Spurs star Alf Ramsey, Ipswich had steadily crept into title contention, and a 3–1 win against Spurs gave them the inner belief to push on and, ultimately, it was to be the East Anglian club that clinched the title by three points from Burnley, with Spurs a point further back in third. It was disappointing for Tottenham that they could not quite hang on to their league crown, as for the most part, they had produced the same brilliant brand of football that had swept all before them the season previously. As well as the obvious determination from opponents to raise their level of play when facing Spurs, the main difference between the two seasons was the form of Tottenham away from White Hart Lane. Clubs all over the country wanted a crack at Spurs, and support from opposition fans was raised to new levels when Spurs were on their travels. Compared with sixteen wins, a draw and four defeats away from home in the 'double' season, Spurs won only seven, drew six and lost eight in the 1961/62 season. In addition, the number of league goals scored away from home was virtually halved, going from 50 to 29.

They may have lost their grip on the league title but, playing as well as ever on the road to Wembley, Spurs held every chance of retaining their FA Cup crown. After a dramatic first encounter in a third round tie at Birmingham, where Spurs had led 3–0 before eventually drawing the game 3–3, Tottenham progressed in the replay, winning 4–2 at White Hart Lane. A trip to the South-West resulted in a 5–1 victory at Plymouth Argyle in the fourth round and West Bromwich Albion were dispatched 4–2 at The Hawthorns a round later. The biggest home crowd of the season (with the exception of the European Cup semi-final second leg clash with Benfica) turned out to see Spurs play Aston Villa in the last eight, and the vast majority went home happy as Spurs enjoyed a surprisingly comfortable 2–0 win over a side that would finish a creditable seventh in the First Division. With the exception of Plymouth, all Tottenham's cup opponents had been First Division clubs, and the trend continued when they were drawn against Manchester United in the semi-final at Hillsborough. United had generally disappointed in their league form, but were expected to raise their game considerably with a trip to Wembley at stake. But Tottenham goals courtesy of Terry Medwin, Greaves and Cliff Jones sent Spurs through for the chance of retaining their trophy, something only Newcastle United had done in the history of Wembley FA Cup finals.

Tottenham Hotspur 3	**Burnley 1**
Greaves, Smith,	Adamson
Blanchflower (pen.)	

Tottenham Hotspur v. Burnley

Smith scores Spurs' second.

It was the unlucky Les Allen that had been the one sacrificed to accommodate Jimmy Greaves when the striker joined from AC Milan, while Medwin had regained the place that he had lost to Terry Dyson during the 'double' season, playing on the right wing with Jones moving to the left. Apart from those two changes, it was the same Spurs side that had beaten Leicester at Wembley the season before. It was league runners-up Burnley that were Tottenham's final opponents. Having finished a place higher than Spurs in the league, many thought Burnley would edge the final too, but Spurs had enjoyed more success in their league meetings, winning 4–2 at White Hart Lane and drawing 2–2 at Turf Moor. Tottenham and Burnley were two well-matched sides and the press anticipated a classic cup final. Burnley possessed some fine individuals expected to trouble Spurs, such as their influential captain Jimmy Adamson, the skilful craftsman Jimmy McIlroy and the bull-like centre forward Ray Pointer.

With just three minutes played, the game erupted into life. Greaves darted through the Burnley defence to reach a flick-on by Bobby Smith and, for a moment, it appeared the ace predator would be clear to run in on goal. But a number of Burnley defenders were quick in their recovery, so Greaves checked to his left. Instinctively shooting with no real sight of goal, the strike caught out the Burnley goalkeeper Adam Blacklaw, and to Greaves' joy the ball roared into the net, sending the Spurs fans hysterical. Both teams carved out opportunities but, rather surprisingly given the attack-minded, open feel to the game, no more goals arrived until the second half. This time it was the Burnley supporters who had their turn to scream their lungs out as, after fifty minutes, a shot by inside left Jimmy Adamson beat Brown in the Spurs goal. The Tottenham section of fans were momentarily stunned into silence but, moments later, the Burnley cheers subsided and it was Spurs in full voice once more as Cliff Jones took John White's pass and crossed to Smith, who slammed the ball viciously past Blacklaw and into the roof of the Burnley net to make it 2–1 to Spurs. With just nine minutes left, Medwin shot from inside the Burnley area and the ball looked destined for the net until defender Tommy Cummings stopped the shot with his hand. Sensing the chance to put Burnley to the sword, Blanchflower stepped up confidently and beat Blacklaw.

The game ended 3–1 and Spurs had won the cup for the fourth time in their history. It had been a long, adventurous, highly entertaining season for Spurs, and they happily celebrated its conclusion as they had done the previous year, as FA Cup winners.

Tottenham Hotspur: Brown, Baker, Henry, Blanchflower, Norman, Mackay, Medwin, White, Smith, Greaves, Jones

Burnley: Blacklaw, Angus, Elder, Adamson, Cummings, Miller, Connolly, McIlroy, Pointer, Robson, Harris

Tottenham Hotspur *v.* Atletico Madrid

Date: 16 May 1963
Location: Rotterdam

Match title: European Cup Winners' Cup final
Attendance: 40,000

The 1962/63 season saw Tottenham continue as a major force in the First Division. Once again their free-flowing, sweeping football was the most attractive in the league and, as in the championship-winning season, the goals followed generously and frequently. In addition, Spurs made a mockery of Ipswich Town's title defence, thrashing the East Anglian side 5–0 at home and 4–2 away. Through all of this, Smith, White, Jones and – most notably – Greaves were scoring at will, dutifully supported by the influential leaders of the side, Blanchflower and Mackay, while also getting some useful contributions from emerging youngster Frank Saul. But, for some reason, this Spurs side did not quite have the air of invincibility that had attached itself to the great 'double' side. They were sent crashing out of the FA Cup at the first hurdle by Burnley and, after a 2–0 win at home to Leyton Orient in late March completed a sequence of eight wins in ten games, Tottenham's league form suddenly deserted them in a most radical manner, losing five and drawing three of their final eleven games. Particularly damaging was the 1–0 reversal against Everton at Goodison Park in April. Everton had emerged as the main rivals for Spurs in the season's title hunt and, from the moment of that match, Everton raised their game to a level Spurs were unable to match, with the Merseyside club winning the title by six points from Spurs.

All was not lost for Tottenham though. They had, the season before, made a bold bid to become the first British side to win a European trophy by reaching the semi-final of the European Cup. This time around, Spurs were entered in the Cup Winners' Cup by virtue of their success in the 1962 FA Cup final. Their first opponents in the competition were Glasgow Rangers, setting up an all-British affair. It was Spurs that outlasted the Scottish giants 8–4 over the two legs and, when the Czech side Slovan Bratislava were readily disposed of in the next round, Spurs faced an encounter with Yugoslavia's OFK Belgrade in the semi-final. The first leg in Yugoslavia saw the home side try to ruffle Tottenham's feathers and disrupt their superior ability by adapting some harsh and at times brutal tactics. Attempting quite literally to kick Spurs out of the competition, their antics produced an angry backlash from some furious Spurs players, notably Bobby Smith and Jimmy Greaves, the latter receiving a rare sending off for retaliation. But Spurs did indeed possess more class and ability and, having ground out a 2–1 victory in Belgrade, Tottenham finished the job in London, a 3–1 win sending them through to their first ever European final. The opposition were Atletico Madrid. Spurs came into the match with a number of injury problems. Dave Mackay and Danny Blanchflower, the heart of the Spurs team, were struggling and, while the latter was declared ready to go having received a painkilling injection shortly before kick-off, Mackay did not make it. His absence was a painful blow for Tottenham, but Nicholson drafted in the capable Tony Marchi to take his place.

The night at Feyenoord's stadium in Rotterdam would go down as one of the greatest nights in Tottenham's history, for not only was it groundbreaking in the result and achievement but it also marked what was probably the crowning moment for this special group of players that made up one of the finest sides of the century. Certainly Spurs would have other memorable results to follow with the core of Nicholson's side but, with the benefit of hindsight, this game was surely the peak of a fabulous journey. Right from the outset, it was clear

Tottenham Hotspur 5
Greaves (2), Dyson (2),
White

Atletico Madrid 1
Collar

Tottenham Hotspur v. Atletico Madrid

that Spurs were in the mood to exhibit the very best football they had become renowned for and, throughout the game, they served up their full repertoire – fluid passing and movement, skill and creativity, resolute and intelligent defending, and above all a determination to take the game to Madrid. With only fifteen minutes on the clock, Cliff Jones stormed in towards the Atletico box and cut a ball back to Greaves who dispatched the chance with relish. One of the key battles during the game was Dyson against the Madrid right-back Rivilla. Dyson was generally seen as a hard-working, honest player who would chip in with some valuable goals. However, he had played an important role in Tottenham's march to the 'double' two seasons previously and, on this particular night, it was the little winger's turn to grasp the spotlight from the likes of White, Jones and Greaves, as he turned in arguably the strongest performance of his Tottenham career. Regularly

Blanchflower is chaired off during the post-match celebrations.

making Rivilla's life hell with his play, he was rewarded ten minutes before half-time when he somehow managed to reach a loose ball that was heading out of play and swung over a cross that fell into the path of White, and the Scot then drilled the ball comfortably past a despairing Madinabeytia. Atletico were 2–0 down but contributing to a splendid game, befitting a team that trailed only Real Madrid in the Spanish League and, as they attacked Spurs shortly before the break, a shot from Adelardo seemed sure to reduce the deficit. However, Ron Henry was in the way and although he blocked the shot he did so with his arm, and from the resulting penalty Collar made the score 2–1. Spurs had been pegged back, yet the football they were playing seemed at a different level to Madrid's, and it was Dyson who was to put the game firmly in their favour. Again running Rivilla ragged, Dyson sent over a deep cross, but this one seemed somewhat off target. However, as the ball floated slowly in the air, it became apparent the cross was turning into more of a shot, and with Madinabeytia caught off-guard and only able to palm at the ball, the ball nestled snugly in the net and Spurs were now in control at 3–1. From there on, Spurs generated some of the most beautiful football that this particular side ever played, demoralising the Spanish with their neat, quick and decisive passing and a Dyson cross set up Greaves to grab the fourth before Dyson himself sealed his Man-of-the-Match performance with a superb individual goal; surging down the middle of the field before cracking in an unstoppable long-range effort to close the scoring at 5–1.

Spurs had gloriously become the first British team to win a European trophy and, as captain Danny Blanchflower lifted the cup, it put a seal on the fantastic achievements of a truly magical Spurs side.

Tottenham Hotspur: Brown, Baker, Henry, Blanchflower, Norman, Marchi, Jones, White, Smith, Greaves, Dyson

Atletico Madrid: Madinabeytia, Rivilla, Griffa, Rodriguez, Ramiro, Glaria, Jones, Adelardo, Chuzo, Mendonca, Collar

Tottenham Hotspur v. Aston Villa

Date: 19 March 1966

Location: White Hart Lane

Match title: Football League First Division

Attendance: 28,290

By the start of the 1965/66 season, the Tottenham Hotspur team was much changed from the great team of the early 1960s that had won the league championship, two FA Cups and a European Cup Winner's Cup. Legendary skipper Danny Blanchflower had retired following the 1963/64 season, with injuries bringing to an end the playing career of one of the greatest players in the club's history. Some, like Bill Brown and Peter Baker had seen new faces come in to take their places, the former's spot taken by the brilliant Pat Jennings and the latter's by emerging full-back Cyril Knowles, while long-serving Ron Henry was no longer in the side after a decade of fine service to the team. Bobby Smith had left for Brighton, Les Allen for QPR and Terry Dyson for Fulham, while centre half Maurice Norman had broken his leg so severely in pre-season that he would never play again. But, most tragically, John White was killed in a freak incident in the summer of 1964. Playing golf in Enfield in July of that year, White sought shelter under a tree during a thunderstorm when it was struck by lightning, killing the Spurs star. At just twenty-six, White's loss was devastating.

Of that great side of the early 1960s, Cliff Jones was still at Spurs but had been plagued by injury since 1965. Dave Mackay was still going strong and was now captain while Jimmy Greaves was still scoring regularly, but by and large it was a totally new side that Nicholson had constructed. As well as Jennings and Knowles, other key members of the side Nicholson was building included Alan Mullery, Jimmy Robertson and Alan Gilzean. Signed from Fulham essentially to replace Blanchflower, Mullery struggled at first to win the fans' acceptance, but over time he developed into one of the best all-round midfield players in the country, his game consisting of quick passing, strong tackling, powerful shooting and an important, natural vocal leadership that made him tailor-made to take over from Mackay when the Spurs captain departed for Derby County in 1968. Robertson was a right-winger with searing speed and, while not in the same class as Jones, provided very good service from the wing following his signing from Scottish club St Mirren in 1964. Robertson's fellow Scot Gilzean joined from Dundee in December 1964 and was a natural successor to Bobby Smith, progressing into one of the most loved centre forwards in the club's history, playing 429 games for Spurs. He was equally adept at creating goals as he was at scoring them, striking up a fine understanding with Greaves.

Spurs were again a top-six side in 1963/64 as well as 1964/65 without really threatening to capture the title and, by the 1965/66 season, they had slipped a little further as the team drifted into an obvious rebuilding period. However, one particular match from the last-named season will long be remembered at White Hart Lane: the league fixture with Aston Villa in March 1966. If ever a match merited the well-coined phrase 'a game of two halves', then this was it. The opening quarter of an hour evoked memories of the glorious 'double' days as Spurs steamrollered Villa. Spurs, struggling through a batch of poor form in the league, had been boosted by the recent return of Greaves to the side following a period of absence caused through hepatitis and, from the kick-off, it was clear his return would provide a huge spark for Spurs. In just the second minute it was Greaves who won a corner and, instinctively taking the kick himself, his cross was met by Mackay, whose shot was turned in by the poaching Gilzean. Two other relative newcomers to the Spurs side, Derek Possee and Eddie Clayton,

Tottenham Hotspur 5	Aston Villa 5
Gilzean, Greaves, Saul, Brown, Robertson	Hateley (4), Deakin

TOTTENHAM HOTSPUR *v.* ASTON VILLA

Perhaps the greatest goalkeeper in the club's history, Pat Jennings established himself in the Spurs side in the mid-1960s.

interchanged some delicate passes in midfield before setting up Greaves to gallop clear moments later and, although the forward's first shot was blocked by the Villa goalkeeper Colin Wither, Greaves made no mistake by striking home at the second attempt. It had been a fast and furious start by Spurs but it was to get better as, a few minutes after Greaves' goal, Frank Saul made it 3–0 with a well-placed header. However, it was to be shortly after that when the first indication arrived that it was not all going to be one-way traffic. Since the injury suffered by Maurice Norman, Spurs had struggled to find a replacement of equal capability, and how they must have longed for their former big man in this particular encounter, as playing for Villa was a tall, physical centre forward called Tony Hateley, and it was he who rose above Tottenham's Laurie Brown to power home Villa's first of the game. Brown made amends for being out-jumped by Hateley by scoring Tottenham's fourth and Robertson completed an incredible half for Spurs by meeting Greaves' cross with a diving header, scoring Tottenham's fifth and placing Spurs in a seemingly unassailable lead.

Perhaps sensing a Spurs weakness, Villa changed their tactics in the second half, sending countless high balls into the Tottenham box, predominantly for Hateley. For Spurs, this was when their already suspect defence began to wilt. With Mullery playing in an unaccustomed right-back role and Brown struggling mightily to cope with Hateley, things appeared ominous when Hateley pulled one back, yet even then Tottenham should have been comfortably ahead – certainly the Spurs side of a few years previously would not have caved – but this was a Spurs team in transition and, within five minutes, it was 5–4, Hateley having scored again, with Alan Deakin adding another. Then, with just five minutes remaining, the Villa comeback was completed as winger Allan Baker beat Mullery, crossed, and fittingly it was Hateley who rose like a giant to thump home the equaliser. Mullery atoned for his error by clearing a late Deakin effort off the line but, having been 5–1 ahead at home, the 5–5 result was deeply dissatisfying for Spurs and their fans, despite the excitement of the match.

Spurs would finish eighth at the end of the season and the Villa game had highlighted many of their deficiencies. However, Bill Nicholson is regarded without a shadow of a doubt as the club's finest manager, and it would not be long before his next super side would be complete.

Tottenham Hotspur: Jennings, Mullery, Knowles, Clayton, Brown, Mackay, Robertson, Greaves, Saul, Gilzean, Possee

Aston Villa: Withers, Wright, Aitken, Poutney, Slueenhoek, Tindall, MacEwan, Hamilton, Hateley, Deakin, Baker

TOTTENHAM HOTSPUR v. CHELSEA

Date: 9 May 1967

Location: Wembley Stadium

Match title: FA Cup final

Attendance: 100,000

It is fair to say that, since that memorable night in 1963 when Spurs had crushed Atletico Madrid to win the European Cup Winners' Cup, the side had been pushed into a rebuilding mode as that great side began to break up. In the interim between then and the side of 1966/67, Spurs had never been in danger of becoming a poor team; it was simply that Bill Nicholson had begun the process of retooling his squad and, although not quite up to the near-unmatchable, prolific standards set by the side of the early 1960s, the team that he built enjoyed a highly satisfying season in 1966/67, once more illustrating the craft, wisdom and mastery of Tottenham's greatest ever manager.

Nicholson had signed many of the key players in this team during the previous few seasons, such as the magnificent goalkeeper Pat Jennings, marauding left-back Cyril Knowles, the rapidly improving Alan Mullery and the graceful forward Alan Gilzean. In addition, a number of players had pleasingly emerged from the lower ranks of the club to become important members of the side. But in the summer of 1966, Nicholson swooped for two players who would add – relatively speaking – the final elements to his next fine Spurs side. First came scheming midfield player Terry Venables – a future manager of the team – from London rivals Chelsea, providing a touch more guile to a midfield already boasting strength and character courtesy of Mullery and Dave Mackay. The second signing proved a masterstroke in hindsight. Beating off competition from long-time potential suitors Manchester United, Nicholson forked out £95,000 – then a record for a defender – for Blackburn Rovers' centre half Mike England. Welsh international England was a much-needed replacement for Maurice Norman and was outstanding in the air as well as being highly capable when passing the ball. One of the most pleasing aspects of the 1966/67 season was the form of Jimmy Greaves and the partnership he carved out with Alan Gilzean. Greaves scored 25 league goals in 1966/67, added another 6 in the FA Cup and formed a devastating combination with Gilzean, who scored 21 league and cup goals himself.

Tottenham's league form remained solid throughout the season, but they really came alive after Christmas, incredibly losing just one of their final twenty league games to place themselves directly in the thick of the title hunt. Unfortunately for Spurs, the one game they did lose was away to Manchester United, and the 1–0 defeat was to prove costly as the Lancashire side took the title by four points, Spurs finishing third on goal difference behind Nottingham Forest. But it was in the FA Cup where Spurs were again to enjoy great success. After London rivals Millwall were seen off after two close games in the third round, Portsmouth and Bristol City were both disposed of at White Hart Lane. Spurs were drawn against Second Division Birmingham City in the quarter-final and, after a dreary 0–0 draw at St Andrews, put the Midlands club to the sword 6–0 at White Hart Lane to set up an enticing semi-final with high-flying Nottingham Forest. Spurs were underdogs, but a fantastic Greaves strike and an opportunistic goal by Saul were enough to send Spurs to Wembley, despite Forest grabbing a late consolatory strike. Their opponents were Chelsea, an improving young side that had finished ninth in the top flight. It was the first ever all-London cup final, and Chelsea were managed by the colourful Tommy Docherty and captained by Ron Harris, while they also contained many quality players such as the skilful Charlie Cooke,

---

Tottenham Hotspur 2

Robertson,

Saul

Chelsea 1

Tambling

TOTTENHAM HOTSPUR v. CHELSEA

Jimmy Greaves was signed from AC Milan.

Bobby Tambling and the man who had given Spurs defenders such a rough time when scoring four for Aston Villa the previous season, Tony Hateley. Chelsea were without one very important player in broken-leg victim Peter Osgood, whereas Spurs were minus homegrown defender Phil Beal, yet the match was hyped up to be a classic as Spurs looked to defend their undefeated record in FA Cup finals.

From a neutral perspective, the game would not have appeared a classic by any means, but perhaps more than any of his previous victories, Nicholson's tactics proved decisive on the day. Throughout the season, the half-back pairing of Mullery and Mackay had seen the former play a more defensive role while the latter regularly got forward to support the attack, with the strategy working to great effect. However, the two basically swapped roles in the final, with Mackay shackling the creative talent of Chelsea's Cooke. In fact, the entire Tottenham defence rarely looked troubled, Knowles getting forward in his customary manner on the left and young Joe Kinnear performing at a high level on the right against the Chelsea left-winger Boyle. By common consensus, Alan Mullery was having perhaps his best game for Spurs, and it was he who provided the spark for the opening goal. Coming forward with a powerful surge, no Chelsea player tackled the marauding defender and he was able to get away a fierce shot at goal. In the way of the shot was Harris yet, as the ball struck the Chelsea captain, it fell to Jimmy Robertson who lashed the rebound past Peter Bonetti in the Chelsea goal, and Spurs had taken the lead.

In the second half, another Knowles foray down the left led to John Collins conceding a throw. Mackay launched a ball that was headed on by the impressive Kinnear, and was turned on by Robertson. As the ball reached Frank Saul, the Spurs forward swivelled in an instant and unleashed an unstoppable finish past Bonetti. Spurs had a few more chances, Kinnear instrumental in sending over crosses, but Saul and Gilzean failed to capitalise. There was hardly any time on the clock when Chelsea got their consolation goal. As Jennings tried to clear a deep centre, his punch was uncharacteristically weak, and it was left to Tambling to head into the Spurs net for 2–1. Try as they might, Chelsea could not force an equaliser that, in truth, would have been unjust, and Spurs held on for another FA Cup triumph.

After nearly ten years of service to Tottenham Hotspur Football Club, Dave Mackay went forward to lift the cup, winning his fifth honour as a member of a Spurs team, and adding another memorable chapter to the distinguished history of the club and further enhancing the status of the great Bill Nicholson.

Tottenham Hotspur: Jennings, Kinnear, Knowles, Mullery, England, Mackay, Venables, Robertson, Gilzean, Greaves, Saul

Chelsea: Bonetti, A. Harris, McCreadie, Hollins, Hinton, R. Harris, Cooke, Baldwin, Hateley, Tambling, Boyle

TOTTENHAM HOTSPUR v. ASTON VILLA

Date: 27 February 1971

Location: Wembley Stadium

Match title: League Cup final

Attendance: 100,000

Following their victory over Chelsea in the 1967 FA Cup final, which capped a highly successful season for Spurs, the club's league form again dipped somewhat in subsequent seasons. They finished seventh in 1967/68, sixth in 1968/69 and eleventh in 1969/70. In those three seasons, Tottenham's league goals totals dropped from 70 to 61 to 54, a common trend in a league that was becoming far more physical, resilient and defensively minded than the First Division in the 1950s and early 1960s. Out of necessity Spurs changed too, a fact not lost on Nicholson as he went about constructing what was to be considered a third memorable side during his reign. The last links to the 'double' side departed – firstly the legendary Dave Mackay, who joined Brian Clough's Derby County and promptly led them to the Second Division title, and then finally Cliff Jones was allowed to join Fulham. Jimmy Greaves, the leading goalscorer in the club's history, also moved on, whether he had wanted to or not in 1970, with the skilful England World Cup-winning midfielder Martin Peters coming the other way from West Ham as part of the deal. The tall, talented centre forward Martin Chivers was signed from Southampton and he soon established himself as a marksman of the highest quality, while pushing through from the younger ranks were decent players such as right-back Ray Evans, central defender Terry Naylor, midfielder John Pratt and winger Jimmy Neighbour, as well as Peter Collins, a bargain signing from Chesterfield and one viewed as a long-term replacement for Mike England. Also coming through at this time was young midfielder Steve Perryman. Tenacious, ambitious, able to play in the 'Tottenham way' and extremely versatile (he would later move to full-back), Perryman would later become Tottenham's all-time appearance leader, club captain and winner of six medals at the club.

Chivers and Peters were quality newcomers and Perryman would go on to cast his name in the Tottenham record books, while the remainder of the 'new blood' were far from exceptional players but certainly offered Spurs a level of industry and competitiveness, fitting the plan that Nicholson had envisioned for his latest Tottenham side. The plan obviously worked for, although Spurs never threatened to become league champions, it was this group of players that formed the backbone of the teams that reached four cup finals (two League and two UEFA) between 1970/71 and 1973/74. The first of this quartet of finals came during the 1970/71 campaign in the League Cup. Spurs had initially snubbed the competition when it was conceived in the early 1960s, and the club's first participation in the competition had arrived in 1966. But they went all the way to Wembley in 1970/71, with the draw kind to them throughout the competition. In the second and third rounds, lower league clubs Swansea City and Sheffield United were seen off at White Hart Lane while struggling First Division outfit West Brom were crushed 5–0 in round four, with Peters scoring a hat-trick. It was Martin Chivers' turn to score three in the next round, as Coventry City were beaten 4–0, again at home. Of the four teams then left in the competition, only Spurs and Manchester United represented the top flight, and the two avoided each other for another round, Spurs being drawn away to Bristol City. The lower league club put up a real fight, earning a highly creditable 1–1 draw at Ashton Gate while, in the replay at White Hart Lane, Spurs were pushed to their limits before extra-time strikes from Chivers and Jimmy Pearce saw them through to Wembley. Surprisingly, it was Third Division Aston Villa that progressed to play Spurs in the final, making Tottenham overwhelming favourites to win

---

Tottenham Hotspur 2

Chivers (2)

Aston Villa 0

Martin Chivers slides home the opening goal.

their first League Cup crown. Five players remained from Tottenham's last visit to Wembley four years previously: Jennings, Kinnear, Knowles, Mullery and Gilzean, although it would have been six had Mike England not been injured (Collins took his place). At just nineteen, Steve Perryman was the youngest player in the Spurs side. It was to be a most disappointing final from a neutral perspective, and even Spurs fans brought up on the tradition of attacking football played in style must have wondered what had become of the rich traditions of their team, so dire was the creative aspect of their play.

The longer the game went on, the more it seemed possible that Villa may cause an upset, as Spurs were not at the races and the Midlands club grew in confidence and composure. After an hour, perhaps the turning point of the match arrived. Playing at centre forward for Villa was the tough and experienced Andy Lockhead, and it was he who went up for a high ball in the Spurs box with Jennings and Collins. Appearing to foul Collins, no whistle was blown and, as the ball broke loose, Lockhead somehow managed to prod the ball towards goal. The Villa fans were on their feet willing and roaring the ball over the line, and even their players began celebrating a near-certain goal, but Perryman had not given up and, from some way off the incident, screamed back to clear the danger and hook the ball away for a throw-in. The scare certainly jolted Spurs and from there they came to life, with the new skipper Mullery rallying his troops. Gilzean made a move forward on seventy-nine minutes before releasing left-winger Neighbour, whose shot was parried by Dunn in the Villa goal. Waiting like a starved hyena was Chivers, who was in exactly the right place to stroke the rebound home to give Spurs the lead. Then, on eighty-two minutes, Chivers made the game safe with a fine individual effort. Outmanoeuvring numerous defenders in the Villa box, he carved himself an opening and hammered the ball past a despairing Dunn.

The second strike by Chivers was the straw that broke the camel's back and was the culmination of a steady rise to fan-favouritism for the former Southampton man. Having joined the club in 1968, Chivers had suffered initially from poor form and then from a knee injury. But with Greaves now gone and supported by Gilzean and Peters, Chivers really came into his own. He would score 174 goals for Spurs, 29 in this particular season alone, and his goals in the 1971 League Cup final earned Spurs a hard-fought 2–0 victory, giving Bill Nicholson his sixth honour as manager of Tottenham and ensuring that the club remained unbeaten in Wembley finals.

Tottenham Hotspur: Jennings, Kinnear, Knowles, Mullery, Collins, Beal, Gilzean, Perryman, Chivers, Peters, Neighbour

Aston Villa: Dunn, Bradley, Aitken, Godfrey, Turnbull, Tiler, McMahon, Rioch, Lochhead, Hamilton, Anderson (Gibson)

TOTTENHAM HOTSPUR v. WOLVERHAMPTON WANDERERS

Date: 17 May 1972

Location: White Hart Lane

Match title: UEFA Cup final 2nd leg

Attendance: 54,303

Although Tottenham's league form was beginning to become a little erratic by the 1971/72 season, it was clear that this particular side had no equal when it came to the one-off occasions of cup football. Spurs went deep into three competitions and could very well have ended up winning all three, but they lost a dramatic, two-legged League Cup semi-final 5–4 to London rivals Chelsea and were narrowly beaten in their FA Cup quarter-final, 2–1, by a Leeds United side that had not finished outside of the top two in the First Division since the 1967/68 season. But it was the UEFA Cup (formerly the Fairs Cup) that brought Tottenham and their supporters their biggest and most rewarding adventure of the season. The team was generally a settled one throughout the season with just one big-name signing joining for the campaign – Ralph Coates and his infamous 'comb-over' hairdo joined from Burnley for £190,000 to provide some extra spice to the midfield and wide areas. Captain Alan Mullery had been absent with a pelvic injury since October 1971 and was later loaned out to Fulham to try and regain his fitness but, in the later stages of the competition, he was recalled and subsequently played a key part in the conclusion.

The UEFA Cup campaign began in September 1971 with a trip to Iceland to play Keflavik. It was perhaps the most straightforward tie in Tottenham's European history, as Alan Gilzean netted a hat-trick in the first leg with Martin Chivers matching his teammate's achievement in the second leg as Spurs won 15–1 on aggregate. Chivers in particular would go on to enjoy a most memorable season, scoring 42 times in all competitions, including 8 in the UEFA Cup matches. Next came a much more competitive game against Nantes, with the only goal coming in the second leg at White Hart Lane from Martin Peters as the French side were ousted. The bad-tempered Romanians of Rapid Bucharest were beaten 5–0 on aggregate, although Jimmy Pearce was sent off for fighting in Romania, while another Romanian side, UT Arad, were beaten 3–1 on aggregate in the quarter-final. In the semi-final Spurs drew a most glamorous tie, yet also a severe test, in the form of Italy's AC Milan. With a typical Italian attitude to breaking-up play – stop first, defend second – Milan were always going to be difficult to beat, and Tottenham's task was made even harder when Romeo Benetti cracked home the opener for the Italians in the first leg at White Hart Lane. But Spurs fought back and it was an unlikely source that won them the day, as young Steve Perryman scored two long-range goals to put Spurs 2–1 ahead for the journey to Milan. The match in the San Siro was a wonderful occasion for Spurs and, boosted by the return of Mullery (who was an inspiration on the night), Spurs fought like dogs, and fittingly it was Mullery who scored the goal that gave Spurs the confidence to cope with Milan's more adventurous home philosophy. The Italians did equalise, but Spurs held on and were through to the final.

Having seen off one of the finest names in European football, the realisation that Spurs were to face their compatriots Wolves in the final was something of an anticlimax for players and supporters alike. Wolves had seen off Hungary's Ferencvaros in their semi-final, but the fact that the Midlands club had finished ninth in the First Division (Spurs finished sixth) made them underdogs in the final. The first leg at Molineux was tight but entertaining. Both sides were intent on getting a positive result to take to White Hart Lane, and chances were

---

Tottenham Hotspur 1

Mullery

Wolverhampton Wanderers 1

Wagstaffe

TOTTENHAM HOTSPUR v. WOLVERHAMPTON WANDERERS

Mullery dives bravely to head the winning goal past Wolves goalkeeper Phil Parkes as Alan Gilzean (right) looks on.

scarce. For Spurs, the two stars of the game were Pat Jennings and Martin Chivers. Jennings made a string of fine saves as Wolves attacked with vigour, but it was Spurs that took the lead with a power header by Chivers. Wolves did find an equaliser but Spurs – soaking up the pressure – hit Wolves late on when Chivers blasted in an absolute thunderbolt from long range to give the men in white a 2–1 lead going into the home leg.

White Hart Lane was rumbling with atmosphere two weeks later as Spurs looked to become the first British side to win different European trophies. Bill Nicholson had not been overly impressed with the manner in which Spurs had gained the result at Molineux, but the important thing was that they had managed to pull out a win, and a steady performance at home would surely earn them the prize. After half an hour, Tottenham's grip on the trophy seemed secure. Having won a free-kick, Martin Peters delivered a cross that was bravely headed home by Mullery, who stepped in front of the onrushing Wolves 'keeper Phil Parkes to register what would be his crowning moment as a Spurs player. Spurs may have thought they had done enough, but Wolves were gritty and refused to give in. A powerful long-range effort from David Wagstaffe brought them back into it just before half-time and, after the interval, Spurs were made to fight for their lives. It would not have been unjustified had Wolves found their second goal that would have taken the game to extra time but, again protected by the excellent Jennings, the Spurs defence held firm, and the crowd went wild with joy at the final whistle.

The Spurs team of the early 1970s had now won their second cup competition and the hero of the day was captain Alan Mullery, who proved he could come back from a serious injury to perform at such a level. Mullery, a fine servant to the club from 1964, was richly deserving of his finest moment, his goal proving to be the decisive factor in the 3–2 scoreline, and he was chaired round the pitch in glorious post-match scenes. Nobody knew it then, but Mullery had played his last game for Spurs and was soon to be sold to Fulham. Martin Peters, the most experienced of the remaining squad members, took Mullery's place as captain.

Tottenham Hotspur: Jennings, Kinnear, Knowles, Mullery, England, Beal, Gilzean, Perryman, Chivers, Peters, Coates

Wolverhampton Wanderers: Parkes, Shaw, Taylor, Hegan, Munro, McAlle, McCalliog, Hibbitt (Bailey), Richards, Dougan (Curran), Wagstaffe

TOTTENHAM HOTSPUR v. NORWICH CITY

Date: 3 March 1973

Location: Wembley Stadium

Match title: League Cup final

Attendance: 100,000

If their league form continued to falter to the concern of many, few could argue with the ability Spurs had to produce consistently in the cup competitions. In the 1972/73 season Tottenham managed a final position of eighth in the league, but both the UEFA Cup and League Cups again produced thrilling campaigns for the supporters as Spurs reached a third major final in three years.

In the UEFA Cup Spurs supporters enjoyed trips to Norway, Greece, Yugoslavia and Portugal before a semi-final date with league champions in waiting Liverpool. Despite Martin Peters scoring twice in the second leg at White Hart Lane, Steve Heighway scored for Liverpool, and with a 1–0 win at Anfield already achieved, coupled with a future Spurs goalkeeper – Ray Clemence – performing at an inspired level, it was the Reds that progressed to the final, breaking Tottenham hearts courtesy of the away-goal rule. But, whereas in the season before Spurs had lost in the semi-final of the League Cup and reached the final of the UEFA Cup, the roles were reversed on this occasion. The early rounds of the competition had seen Spurs paired with lower league clubs Huddersfield Town, Middlesbrough and Millwall, with Middlesbrough causing real problems, playing out two tight draws before Spurs finally progressed in a third match 2–1. The fifth round threw forward a thoroughly difficult test for Spurs, with Liverpool the opponents at Anfield. But Spurs played well away, drawing 1–1, and in the replay Spurs turned on the style in perhaps their best performance of the season, with two goals by Martin Chivers and another from John Pratt seeing them through 3–1. The semi-final was almost a carbon copy of the previous season's UEFA Cup final as Spurs always just had the edge in a two-legged affair with Wolves. Made to fight all the way to the death, Spurs eventually made it through 4–3 on aggregate. Having accounted for Chelsea in the other semi-final, Norwich City had emerged to take their place at Wembley for the first time. The Canaries were fighting relegation in the First Division and Spurs were heavily fancied to win. Although Alan Mullery had moved on to Fulham, the Spurs side revolved around the same group of players that had featured in finals the previous two years. The in-form John Pratt, a substitute for the UEFA Cup final clashes with Wolves the year before, had replaced Mullery in midfield and had scored a marvellous goal in the first leg of the semi-final.

Right from the off it was clear that Norwich manager Ron Saunders only had one objective for the final, and that was to stop Spurs from playing football. Packing their entire team behind the ball at times, Norwich defended in vast numbers, limiting the space and time Spurs had on the ball. As a spectacle it was dire, but even though Norwich showed no trace of adventure in their attacking play, by the same token, Spurs' perceived 'big' players such as Peters, Gilzean and Chivers were having poor games, and Tottenham as a team looked lethargic and out of sync. Pratt, starting his first final of any description for Spurs, suffered the huge disappointment of being injured early on in the game, and he cut a disconsolate figure as he left the pitch. On in his place after a mere twenty-five minutes came Ralph Coates.

The game (unfortunately for all concerned) appeared to be drifting towards extra time until the crucial moment of the match arrived on seventy-two minutes. A Spurs throw-in was flicked on in the Canaries area by Peters, but was then blocked away by the Norwich defender David Cross. Lurking on the edge of the box was Coates.

Tottenham Hotspur 1

Coates

Norwich City 0

Match winner Ralph Coates with the cup.

Seizing on the loose ball, he was able to drill a shot past Keelan in goal and into the bottom-left corner of the net. Coates started off on a joyous celebration dance, accompanied by a massive sigh of relief from the Spurs fans (and most likely all neutrals too).

Coates' strike was enough to win the game, yet it had hardly been a case of Spurs winning the cup, merely playing slightly less poorly than Norwich in one of the worst Wembley finals ever. But another honour had been added to the Tottenham Hotspur trophy cabinet, and the early 1970s side had now won three trophies, and that was something to be extremely proud of.

Tottenham Hotspur: Jennings, Kinnear, Knowles, Pratt (Coates), England, Beal, Gilzean, Perryman, Chivers, Peters, Pearce

Norwich City: Keelan, Payne, Stringer, Forbes, Butler, Briggs, Livermore, Paddon, Anderson, Blair (Howard), Cross

Tottenham Hotspur v. Feyenoord

Date: 21 May 1974

Location: White Hart Lane

Match title: UEFA Cup final 1st leg

Attendance: 46,281

There was no denying that Tottenham's league form and general style of play of the previous few seasons was starting to become an issue for their supporters. It was no coincidence that they were becoming less attractive to watch and that the big-name signings of previous years seemed few and far between. The fans had certainly noticed, and this reflected in some of the home attendance figures. When Stoke City visited White Hart Lane in December 1973, only 14,034 fans turned up, the lowest league crowd for twenty years. Bill Nicholson too was becoming disenchanted, not only with how his current Spurs side played (a somewhat less graceful, more physical style than Nicholson's early Spurs teams, although some of this was at his insistence so as to adapt to the way English football had developed in the 1970s) but also with football in general, believing money and player power were overshadowing his once-cherished philosophy of style, team-play and commitment to winning.

For the first time since the 1958/59 season, Spurs lost as many league games as they won and, in a First Division dominated by Leeds United and the emerging force of English football Liverpool, Tottenham could only finish eleventh in the table and also went out of the FA Cup and League Cup competitions at the first time of asking.

The team seemed destined for a transitional period, despite the great cup exploits of previous seasons. Peters and Chivers remained the class players in the side but were not getting any younger; the same was true of Mike England at the back while Alan Gilzean was playing his final season for the club and was in and out of the side. The team had a more industrious feel to it than ever before; willing workers like Perryman and Pratt, although admirable in their toiling, were often ridiculed by the fans for simply not being in the class of Blanchflower, White or Mackay. This seemed particularly unfair in the case of Perryman, a staunch performer and loyal contributor for Spurs who definitely had creative ability but was given the less glamorous role of midfield destroyer in Nicholson's Spurs team, a fact that did not always please the man who would go on to play the most games for Tottenham in the club's history. Ray Evans and Terry Naylor had come in to the side as full-backs, and the likes of Phil Holder and Mike Dillon, graduates from the youth side, had been given their chances when no new names arrived. There were bright spots however; Jennings continued in magnificent form in goal and young winger Chris McGrath, only eighteen, had broken into the side and was beginning to demonstrate his raw skills, proving especially effective in what would turn into a sensational run in the UEFA Cup.

In truth, if it had not been for the UEFA Cup, the 1973/74 season would have been cast aside as a total disappointment for Spurs. The first four rounds brought an abundance of goals, but also a feeling that these performances were masking some long-term deficiencies in the side. Grasshoppers of Switzerland were beaten 9–2 on aggregate, Aberdeen 5–2, Dinamo Tbilisi of Georgia 6–2, and a much-vaunted Cologne side (including top German goalkeeper Harald Schumacher) 5–1. Chivers and Peters, as one would expect, were among the goals in the early rounds, but the real bonus was the form displayed by McGrath, who scored four goals in these games, including a fine individual run and strike against Aberdeen at White Hart Lane that really announced his arrival. McGrath was then on target in both legs of Tottenham's semi-final with East Germany's Lokomotiv Leipzig, and Spurs progressed through to their second UEFA Cup final 4–1 on aggregate.

Tottenham Hotspur 2	Feyenoord 2
England,	Van Hanegem,
Van Daele (o.g.)	De Jong

Mike England scored in the first leg at White Hart Lane.

The opposition was extremely tough, and came in the form of the new Dutch champions Feyenoord. Unfortunately for Spurs, the first leg was at home, a factor that is often seen as negative in European ties, and so it proved on this occasion. It was to prove a frustrating night for Spurs although they came out attacking the Dutch side with conviction. A breakthrough appeared likely, and it arrived on thirty-nine minutes when Evans sent over a deep free-kick that was met by the head of Mike England, and the defender's effort soared into the net.

Just as Tottenham's confidence grew, Feyenoord – a dashing, skilful side – were level. Van Hanegem, their outstanding player, clipped a beautiful free-kick past Jennings and the ball went in off a post. The most agonising

Tottenham Hotspur: Jennings, Evans, Naylor, Pratt, England, Beal (Dillon), McGrath, Perryman, Chivers, Peters, Coates

Feyenoord: Treytel, Rijsbergen, Van Daele, Israel, Vos, De Jong, Jansen, Van Hanegem, Ressel, Schoenmaker, Kristensen

A fan arrives back in London having been injured during the violence that marred the second leg in Holland.

aspect of Feyenoord's equaliser from the Tottenham perspective was that it arrived barely moments before the interval, giving the Dutch side a huge boost knowing they had gained the priceless 'away goal'.

Feyenoord certainly came out playing the better football in the second half, but Jennings was in commanding form for Spurs, and it was to be Tottenham that regained the lead. From a similar position to the first goal, Evans again swung over a free-kick and with England causing problems in the area, the unfortunate Van Daele put through his own net.

At 2–1 Spurs would have had a decent chance in the return leg in Rotterdam but, to go in to that game with real belief, a third goal was vital. Spurs carved out a number of chances but Feyenoord stood firm and, devastatingly for Spurs, it was the Dutch who grabbed the final goal of the game very late on, as De Jong broke clear of his marker Perryman, nipped in behind the defence and stole his side a 2–2 draw.

Spurs knew it would be tough going to Rotterdam with a 2–1 lead, but a draw was a bad result. It meant at the very least they had to score in Holland and most likely keep the enterprising Dutch at bay. Early on in the second leg there was real hope for Spurs as Chris McGrath appeared to have scored, but when the goal was disallowed for offside it seemed to act as the beginning of Tottenham's downfall.

In the stands, violence and rioting were taking place. It got so bad that Nicholson was forced to plead to the travelling Spurs fans to stop their awful behaviour through an announcement made over the loudspeaker during the half-time interval.

Feyenoord had scored once in the first half, and in the second they began to control the game, passing the ball around in the style that the Spurs teams of previous years would have been proud of. In the end, Spurs lost the second leg 2–0, and the final 4–2 on aggregate. It was a sad occasion as Spurs lost a major final for the first time, and was made worse by the news that the dreadful antics of the Spurs fans had led to the club being banned from playing their next two European ties at White Hart Lane.

Nicholson seemed affected more than anyone by this. He had built three great sides in his time at Spurs: the side that appeared in four cup finals in the early 1970s, the FA Cup-winning side of 1967 and, unforgettably, the legendary 'double' side of the early 1960s. But in 1974/75, the season after the UEFA Cup final second leg in Rotterdam, the team really began to struggle. Spurs got off to a dreadful start in the league and, not long into the season, Bill Nicholson resigned. He had been the greatest manager Spurs had ever had and were ever likely to have, and when he passed away many years later in 2004, thousands of supporters, ex-players and members of the present-day team turned up at White Hart Lane for a most fitting memorial service.

It was Danny Blanchflower who Nicholson wanted most to succeed him, but the Spurs board opted for Terry Neill, manager of Hull City. Neill struggled mightily in that first season, avoiding relegation by a mere point. Although results improved somewhat the next season (Spurs finished ninth), Neill was not delivering the kind of football the fans relished, and he too resigned in the summer of 1976. In came the quiet Yorkshireman Keith Burkinshaw, and a new era began at Spurs.

TOTTENHAM HOTSPUR v. LEEDS UNITED

Date: 28 April 1975

Location: White Hart Lane

Match title: Football League First Division

Attendance: 49,886

It was always going to be a tough situation for Terry Neill when he was appointed as manager of Spurs when Bill Nicholson was allowed to leave at the beginning of the 1974/75 season. Being a former captain of Tottenham's bitter north London rivals Arsenal was bad enough in terms of respect and admiration from the supporters, but the fact that the period from the mid to late 1970s produced some of the poorest and most disappointing Tottenham sides in club history made his job doubly tough. On taking over from Nicholson, Neill initially seemed to spark the team as they won games against West Ham and Wolves, but then followed a disastrous mid-season slump when the club lost thirteen games between December and April.

As well as realising that the fans would never truly accept him, Neill seemed to fall out with a number of the more senior players at the club, notably Martin Peters and Mike England, both of whom were allowed to leave before the season was over. In return, Neill signed tough-tackling defender Don McAllister from Bolton Wanderers and striker John Duncan – prolific if ungraceful – from Dundee. In addition, Neill presented first-team opportunities to a number of the club's most promising youngsters in talented central defender Keith Osgood and sharp forward Chris Jones, as well as introducing into the team one of Nicholson's last signings, Scotland's Alfie Conn, an attacking talent of unlimited potential yet a player who was just as likely to delight with a burst of sheer brilliance as he was to frustrate through lack of commitment to team play or through crazy, irresponsible antics.

In their first season without the greatest manager in the club's history, it was certainly a case of 'after the Lord Mayor's show' and, as the season deteriorated at a rapid pace, it soon became obvious that this great club were fighting for their First Division lives. A defeat at Arsenal – who were not enjoying the greatest season themselves – left Spurs in dire straights heading into the last game of the season. Carlisle United were already relegated, but two more from Spurs, Luton Town and Chelsea were facing the drop as well and this meant that, to be sure of staying in the top flight, Spurs would have to beat Leeds United at White Hart Lane. Although Liverpool had taken over from Leeds as the powerhouse of the First Division, the Yorkshire side, managed by Don Revie, were still a match for anyone, as their progression to that season's European Cup final proved. However, much-criticised by the media for being too fickle in times of adversity, the Spurs fans provided an emphatic and rousing display of support for their team on this day, with nearly 50,000 packing into White Hart Lane in an effort to roar their team to safety. On the day, the team did not let their fans down.

Leeds had not come close to defending the title they had won the season before, but they remained a very tough proposition, hard and uncompromising, and any chance that they would simply roll over and let Spurs cruise to safety was non-existent. However, this was a day when Tottenham's faltering side were inspired, coming good when it mattered. There were fighters in the Spurs side too, and any thoughts of the likes of Kinnear, Naylor, Perryman and Chivers giving up their top-flight status easily were blown out of the window after just five minutes. It was to be one of the club's longest-serving players, Cyril Knowles, who was to be the star of the night. For so long a fan favourite with his surging runs from left-back, it was Knowles' killer left foot that struck home a vicious free-kick to open the scoring, White Hart Lane exploding in joy while breathing a collective sigh

Tottenham Hotspur 4	Leeds United 2
Knowles (2, 1 pen.),	Jordan,
Chivers, Conn	Lorimer

Tottenham Hotspur v. Leeds United

of relief at the same time. For the remainder of the first half, Spurs threw caution to the wind, attacking in eye-catching style, but similarly knowing that any mistakes in defence would put their First Division status in jeopardy. Tottenham had to be given credit for their determination to try and kill off the Leeds threat, while the visitors could be equally praised for their stubbornness not to cave in under constant pressure.

But as the Spurs attacks continued in the second half, a second, precious goal was not far away for Spurs. Chivers – sorely missed because of injury for the previous two months – stabbed home from a short distance to make it 2–0. Then, not long after, Spurs really started to enjoy themselves. Trevor Cherry chopped down Perryman in the Leeds area, and up stepped Knowles to convert the penalty and confirm himself as the hero of the day. Although Jordan grabbed a goal for Leeds to cast a momentary shadow of doubt, the goal of the game – and the safety-clinching goal – arrived soon afterwards from

Alfie Conn scored a vital goal against Leeds.

the unpredictable, controversial but unquestionably gifted Alfie Conn, who had become something of a cult figure among the Spurs fans with his long, shoulder-length hair and a hat-trick on his debut against Newcastle in January. Surging in mesmerising style through a host of Leeds defenders, Conn scored Tottenham's fourth to spark incredible scenes of rejoicing on the terraces. Illustrating his bizarre nature, Conn then proceeded to taunt the visiting supporters, perhaps unwisely given his inconsistent time at Tottenham, by sitting on the ball. Peter Lorimer snatched a late consolation for Leeds but it mattered not, Spurs had avoided the drop and, in times of change, restructuring and occasional lack of harmony at White Hart Lane, the result was treated as gratefully and celebrated as boldly as any big-match success in recent seasons, and the relieved and ecstatic fans invaded the pitch at the end of the game to swamp the players.

Of course, a last-day victory to disguise a season of disappointment did not bode well for the future. Tottenham's league form had been declining for a number of years now and, although results picked up a little the season after when they finished ninth, Neill jumped ship for neighbours Arsenal to become their manager. In truth, Neill never really got on with the board, always performing – perhaps unfairly – in the shadow of Bill Nicholson, yet he was certainly not a popular manager with the Spurs fans, who pined for a return to the days of seeing football played the way they loved. Charged with restoring past glories was Keith Burkinshaw, first-team coach under Neill, but a shock appointment in the eyes of many, given that his highest level of experience as a manager had come when in charge of Scunthorpe United. The appointment, in time, was to be a glorious success, but first there would be rough times for Burkinshaw, beginning with his first season in charge.

Tottenham Hotspur: Jennings, Kinnear, Knowles, Beal, Osgood, Naylor, Conn, Perryman, Chivers, Jones, Pratt

Leeds United: Stewart, Reaney, Cherry, Bremner, Madeley, Hunter, Lorimer, F. Gray, Jordan, Yorath, E. Gray

TOTTENHAM HOTSPUR v. BRISTOL ROVERS

Date: 22 October 1977

Location: White Hart Lane

Match title: Football League Second Division

Attendance: 26,311

It was always going to be a tough task for Keith Burkinshaw in his first season in charge. Most of the mainstays of the successful cup sides of the early 1970s were now gone, including Martin Chivers who had opted for Continental football, joining Servette in Switzerland, and Cyril Knowles, who had been forced to retire through injury. Burkinshaw's initial purchases included useful Carlisle United left-back John Gorman, speedy winger Peter Taylor from Crystal Palace and the tall, bearded centre forward Ian Moores from Stoke City. But the new players needed time to settle in at a far bigger club than those that they had left and, as a result, the team began to leak goals alarmingly as the defence all too frequently came under siege. Matters were made worse when Gorman got badly injured, forcing him to miss much of the next two seasons in sporadic patches, and Spurs had to sign Coventry City's Jimmy Holmes as an emergency replacement. Tottenham's confidence was visibly ebbing away as the weeks passed and they were on the wrong end of some severe hidings, including an 8–2 reversal at the 1974/75 champions Derby County and a 5–3 defeat at West Ham. Crushed 5–0 by Manchester City in the penultimate fixture of the season, Spurs looked doomed. Their league form had been woeful for a number of years and they failed to escape their destiny of relegation despite a last-day victory over Leicester, sadly dropping into the Second Division together with Stoke City and Sunderland.

Although they had witnessed a dismal campaign, the Spurs fans showed outstanding loyalty and support to the players as news of their relegation became apparent. What Burkinshaw needed was time to mould his side and get them playing in the well-intentioned way he desired. He had a good base with captain Steve Perryman, a tough-tackling but intelligent player with unquestionable commitment to the Tottenham cause. He had one good young midfielder capable of playing the 'Tottenham way' in Neil McNabb and a potentially great one in Glenn Hoddle. He also had a fast, skilful – if sometimes confidence-lacking – winger in Taylor and he had a batch of more experienced workers who would be more than useful in the fight to climb out of the Second Division in the likes of Terry Naylor, Don McAllister and John Pratt.

Although much-criticised for the decision to let Pat Jennings leave for Arsenal in favour of long-time reserve Barry Daines, Spurs showed from the outset that they were going to be the class proposition in the Second Division. With Hoddle developing into the key component in midfield, the team got off to a flyer, winning five of their first seven games before a surprise loss at Hull City in October. In the weeks leading up to Christmas, the team really hit their stride, gradually buying into the Burkinshaw way of playing, and scoring goals by the bucket-load. The most memorable game of the season came towards the end of October in a home date with Bristol Rovers. Just two days before the game, Burkinshaw had paid Torquay United £60,000 for Colin Lee, a tall, relatively unknown centre forward. If the Spurs fans knew little of Lee before the game, then they certainly knew who he was afterwards, as Lee enjoyed a debut that even superseded that of Jimmy Greaves for its emphatic nature. Spurs had lost 4–1 against Charlton in the previous game, but they showed tremendous resilience against Rovers, treating the smallish crowd at White Hart Lane to a goal feast and a performance of pure domination that raised spirits considerably for the battle for promotion that lay ahead.

Tottenham Hotspur 9

Lee (4), Taylor,
Moores (3), Hoddle

Bristol Rovers 0

Tottenham Hotspur v. Bristol Rovers

It may have been the newcomer Lee who stole the headlines in this game, but the emerging star of the side was the supremely gifted Hoddle and, on the day before his twentieth birthday, he destroyed Rovers with his craft, vision and skill. After twenty-one minutes Hoddle's cross was drilled home by Lee, giving the striker the perfect start to his Spurs career, and on twenty-five minutes he had doubled his total as he met John Pratt's corner with a thumping header. Moments before the interval, Hoddle was the architect once more, crossing for Taylor to get on the scoresheet. The second half saw Spurs simply annihilate Rovers. Ian Moores joined in on the goalscoring act just before the hour mark and it was not long before Lee achieved his debut hat-trick, much to the delight of his teammates. Moores too was to register a hat-trick, notching two quick-fire strikes in succession, before Lee scored an astonishing fourth goal on eighty-eight minutes. Lee's goals were made all the more astounding due to the fact that he was formerly a defender and had only been playing as a striker at Torquay for a short while and, when he joined

Spurs v. Bristol Rovers, 1977.

Chelsea few seasons later, he again switched to defence. Inevitably, after such an awesome beginning to his life at Tottenham, nothing Lee could do in a white shirt came close to matching his stunning debut, and he scored only seven more goals that season and ended up with 21 in total in his 65-game Spurs career. Bristol Rovers had been well and truly demoralised, but there was still time for one more goal and, fittingly, it came from Hoddle. Scorching through the visitors' defence to collect a long pass from Moores, Hoddle tucked the ball away calmly and Spurs had won 9–0.

The victory sent Spurs surfing a confidence wave, which they rode to the latter stages of the season, losing just once more before April and looking assured of promotion. Then came a stretch in April when they lost three games out of four and, with Bolton Wanderers already up as champions, Spurs needed to avoid defeat against Southampton on the final day to go up. The teams drew 0–0 at The Dell and both Saints and Spurs were promoted with Brighton – who had beaten Spurs 3–1 two weeks previously – the unlucky side to miss out. Promoted they were, but Burkinshaw needed to recruit more class if they were going to maintain their position in the top flight. At the end of the season, Argentina won the 1978 World Cup on their home soil and, when Spurs captured two of their players in a blockbuster deal, the club were thrown seriously into the limelight. The two players in question were the diminutive but gloriously talented playmaker Osvaldo Ardiles and the big, black-bearded Ricardo Villa, a player of real flair but something of an unknown having made just two substitute appearance in Argentina's march to glory. The capable centre half John Lacy was also signed, from Fulham, and Spurs recommenced in the First Division with real optimism.

Tottenham Hotspur: Daines, Naylor, Holmes, Hoddle, McAllister, Perryman, Pratt, McNabb, Moores, Lee, Taylor

Bristol Rovers: Jones, Bater, T. Taylor, Day, S. Taylor, Prince (Hendrie), Williams, Aitken, Gould, Staniforth, Evans

TOTTENHAM HOTSPUR v. MANCHESTER UNITED

Date: 9 January 1980

Location: Old Trafford

Match title: FA Cup third round replay

Attendance: 53,762

The Argentine World Cup winners obviously created a lot of attention for Spurs, the swoop for the pair being described by many as the transfer of the decade, and went a long way towards silencing those critics who had accused Tottenham of no longer attracting the big, star players. But for two seasons, the art of integrating two South American footballers into a side trying to re-establish itself in the First Division was very troublesome for Burkinshaw as he strove to find the correct balance for his team. Although Ardiles and, eventually, Villa settled to life in England, it was not always a smooth transition on the pitch. On the opening day of the 1978/79 season, Spurs drew 1–1 with Nottingham Forest beneath a baking sun, with Villa signalling his arrival with a wonderful goal. Much was expected when the World Cup winners made their home debuts against Aston Villa, but it did not take long to realise that simply putting the two into the midfield and letting them get on with it was going to encounter its share of difficulties and a steep period of adjustment for both the Argentinians and their new teammates. Spurs were thumped 4–1 by Villa and, ten days later, were crushed 7–0 by Liverpool at Anfield. Even so, Spurs managed to finish eleventh in their first season back among the big boys, with Burkinshaw always encouraging football in the Spurs tradition. Things continued in much the same way the season after; up and down results in the league, structural problems within the side, some good football, some exposed defensive frailties but a strong insistence from the unflappable Burkinshaw that Spurs were on the right track.

One of the most exciting encounters of those first two seasons back in the First Division came against Manchester United in the third round of the FA Cup in 1980 and gave an indication to fans of a bright, not too distant future in the competition for Spurs. United were title challengers in this particular season, emerging as the biggest threat to the domination of the seemingly unstoppable Liverpool machine. They had in their ranks, among others, the tough Scottish centre half Gordon McQueen, as well as a talented group of midfield and forward players including Steve Coppell, Ray Wilkins, Lou Macari and Joe Jordan. United had beaten Spurs 2–1 at White Hart Lane in the league, would beat them again 4–1 at Old Trafford in April, and had put Spurs out of the League Cup in the second round, 5–2 on aggregate, so they were obviously heavy favourites to earn a positive result in the third round fixture at White Hart Lane. But, inspired by Hoddle and Ardiles, Spurs managed a 1–1 draw, with the Argentine getting Tottenham's goal, but there were few who gave Spurs a chance in the replay at Old Trafford four days later.

If the task was expected to be tough for Spurs from the outset, it suddenly became near impossible when goalkeeper Milija Aleksic, British-born but with a Yugoslav father, had his jaw broken in a collision with the physical United centre forward Joe Jordan. In one of the most memorable images in Spurs' history, Aleksic was taken from the field and replaced by the only substitute, midfielder John Pratt, and Hoddle took up the goalkeeping position. From that moment, Spurs became a resilient force, brave and determined not to be beaten despite their now slim chance of success. Incredibly, Tottenham forced extra time and, as if the script had been written for them, the two Argentinians combined to give Spurs a most unlikely victory. A typical Villa run and dribble took the big midfielder into the United area where he cut the ball back for Ardiles to score his most

---

Tottenham Hotspur 1

Ardiles

Manchester United 0

TOTTENHAM HOTSPUR v. MANCHESTER UNITED

important goal yet in a Spurs uniform. At the final whistle, Spurs rightfully enjoyed a rapturous reception from their travelling fans and, although they eventually bowed out of the competition 1–0 to Liverpool in the quarter-finals, the seeds had been sown for future raids in the FA Cup, a competition that was to capture the hearts of both 'Ossie and Ricky', bringing out the best in the pair.

A final position of fourteenth in the league suggested Burkinshaw still had much to do, but the manager was slowly piecing together his desired team. The key to the midfield was finding the best positions for the Argentinians, and although Ardiles learnt how to cover and defend (improving all the time in that respect), Villa was far more of a free spirit and it was not unusual to see him on the bench. But Burkinshaw learned when best to use Villa and, with Hoddle turning into the most cultured midfielder in England, Spurs could boast an abundance of midfield skill to rival any team in the league. The defence was starting to take shape too; Perryman was switched back to his

Spurs v. Manchester United, 1980.

best position of right-back where he could use his natural competitiveness and desire to join in attacks without omitting one of the midfield stars, while youngsters in centre half Paul Miller and full-back Chris Hughton had come through to earn places in the team.

Going into the 1980/81 season, Burkinshaw added the missing pieces to what would develop into the next great Spurs side. In came bargain-basement defender Graham Roberts – tough, hard but also a fine footballer – from non- league Weymouth, and he soon formed a new-look central defensive partnership with Paul Miller. Strikers Steve Archibald and Garth Crooks – both long-time Burkinshaw targets – joined from Aberdeen and Stoke City respectively, and together formed the best Spurs striking combination since the peak of Chivers and Gilzean, and with the two came the firepower that Spurs had yearned for. The flame-haired Archibald had a fine first touch and a natural goalscorer's instinct, while the panther-quick Crooks proved a handful for the division's defenders, darting into the smallest of spaces to feast on half chances and work as a perfect complement to the more technical Archibald. Additionally, underrated but extremely effective left-winger Tony Galvin (on the brink of the first team before a pelvic injury had ruined his chance the season before) became a regular, giving Spurs real natural width, while home-grown youngsters in centre forward Mark Falco and attacking midfielder Garry Brooke gave the team outstanding depth. The team was headed in the right direction and, for the next four seasons, Burkinshaw was able to bring the glory days – and nights – back to White Hart Lane.

Tottenham Hotspur: Aleksic (Pratt), Hughton, McAllister, Yorath, Miller, Perryman, Ardiles, Armstrong, Gibson, Hoddle, Villa

Manchester United: Unknown

TOTTENHAM HOTSPUR v. WOLVERHAMPTON WANDERERS

Date: 15 April 1981

Location: Highbury

Match title: FA Cup semi-final replay

Attendance: 52,539

It was the 1980/81 season when Burkinshaw's Spurs really began to take off and become the side the manager had envisioned. True, the team was still somewhat inconsistent in the league – as their final finishing position of tenth fully illustrated – but Spurs now possessed (particularly from January 1981 onwards) a far better shape than when they had first returned to the top flight, and their style of play was beginning to come together nicely, particularly in the attacking department where the team now had four or five players at the peak of their powers, plus a batch of tough, young, determined defenders and a veteran leader in captain Steve Perryman to guide them into what would soon become one of the most successful and exciting periods in the club's history. With Hoddle and Ardiles pulling the strings in midfield, the strikers – Archibald and Crooks – found their form from the outset, and both delivered blistering seasons, Archibald netting 25 times in all competitions and Crooks 22. Graham Roberts came into the team around Christmas 1980 and his central defensive partnership with Miller gave Spurs a young, aggressive duo to build from, and the restructuring was complete by January when Tony Galvin forced his way into the line-up to give Spurs a willing left-winger, allowing them to switch Villa to the right side of midfield.

Things were starting to come together as Spurs began their FA Cup run in January. Paired with London neighbours Queens Park Rangers in the third round, it turned out to be a tougher match than expected for Spurs as the lower division side made a real fight of it on their artificial pitch. Some critics suggested Spurs were lucky to escape with a 0–0 draw but, in the replay at White Hart Lane, Spurs showed their class, sweeping to a 3–1 victory with goals from Galvin, Hoddle and Crooks. Hull City were accounted for at home in the fourth round and Coventry City of the First Division were easily beaten a round later as Ardiles shone, scoring once and proving a constant menace to the Midlands side in a 3–1 victory. Exeter City were the perceived weaklings among the final eight teams but, at White Hart Lane, they exceeded themselves, forcing Spurs to pull out all the stops to progress. In the end it took a couple of late goals from centre-backs Miller and Roberts to see Spurs through. Of the four teams remaining in the cup – all from the First Division – Ipswich Town were enjoying by far the strongest season in the league, challenging for the title, while Manchester City, like Spurs, were a good side, capable of beating anyone, but mid-table nonetheless. Wolves were considered the poorest side left and were fighting relegation, and it was they that Spurs were paired with. Spurs went into the game full of confidence, certain the superior skills and intelligent play of Hoddle, Ardiles and the forwards could out-do the physical style Wolves were sure to adopt – in particular the excellent Scottish centre forward Andy Gray.

At Hillsborough, Spurs came out attacking from the get-go and, after just four minutes, Galvin's cross was met on the stretch by Archibald who put Tottenham ahead. Although Wolves responded majestically and equalised shortly after through their clever midfield player Kenny Hibbitt, Spurs generally controlled the game and Hoddle's beautifully placed free-kick restored the lead just before the break. Despite their dominance, Spurs failed to kill the game off and, with just seconds remaining, they quite literally paid the penalty. As Hoddle won the ball from Hibbitt in the Spurs area, the Wolves player went to ground. Astonishingly, referee Clive Thomas gave a penalty

Tottenham Hotspur 3	Wolverhampton Wanderers 0
Crooks (2),	
Villa	

TOTTENHAM HOTSPUR v. WOLVERHAMPTON WANDERERS

Wolves striker Andy Gray takes on Ardiles (left), Hughton and Miller (right) in the semi-final.

to Wolves, infuriating the Spurs players who carried on their protests long after Willie Carr had converted the spot kick. Television replays proved it was a fair tackle by Hoddle, but extra time had been forced and, with Spurs now totally out of sorts and clearly frustrated by what had happened, they were fortunate not to lose, and the game went to a replay. Spurs had let a golden chance of reaching an FA Cup final slip away by not putting Wolves to the sword. But in the replay – ironically at the home of their bitter rivals Arsenal, Highbury – there would be no such let-up.

On a cold, crisp night, Spurs really turned on the style. Gray, Wolves' best player was missing, but Spurs produced a memorable performance to put right the injustice of the first match. Playing so close to their own ground lent great support to Tottenham on the night, with the crowd roaring them on. As in the game at Hillsborough Spurs came out in full flow and, on eleven minutes, Hoddle set up Crooks who headed home a bullet to give Spurs the lead. The same combination hooked up just before the break, Hoddle providing a delightful, killer through-ball on which Crooks pounced like a predator, searing past the Wolves defence to meet the pass and beat Bradshaw in the Wolves goal. Crooks almost had a hat-trick later as he was again through on goal, but instead he set up Archibald, who uncharacteristically missed the chance. But the goal of the night was Tottenham's third and came courtesy of Ricardo Villa. Picking up a pass near the centre circle, Villa ran at the Wolves defence before cutting inside and letting go a rocket of a shot that flew into the top-left corner of the Wolves net. It was a sight that Spurs fans felt should have been more frequent during Villa's stay at White Hart Lane given the player's raw ability but, nevertheless, as the ball met its destination, it was greeted with a thunderous cheer.

Justice had been done. Spurs had won in style, and they were now through to contest a sixth FA Cup final and their first for fourteen years.

Tottenham Hotspur: Aleksic, Hughton, Miller, Roberts, Villa (Brooke), Perryman, Ardiles, Archibald, Galvin, Hoddle, Crooks

Wolverhampton Wanderers: Unknown

TOTTENHAM HOTSPUR v. MANCHESTER CITY

Date: 14 May 1981

Location: Wembley Stadium

Match title: FA Cup final replay

Attendance: 96,000

Tottenham's opponents in the centenary cup final were Manchester City, a side that had struggled at the wrong end of the First Division for much of the season but had been revitalised ever since John Bond had come in as manager to lift their flagging fortunes. Spurs were hotly fancied to win the match, most believing they would have too much for City to cope with. It was the first major platform for Hoddle to perform on and he was expected to shine, while much attention focused on the Argentine duo and a lot was made of Ardiles and his dream to play at Wembley.

All the while Manchester City were generally overlooked, but they were not without talent. The match was billed to be a contrast in styles – pure football against work-rate and power but, on the day, the final proved somewhat disappointing, particularly from a Tottenham point of view. It was not a poor game, more that Spurs simply did not play as they could. The City midfield stifled Hoddle and Ardiles; Hutchinson, Power, Gow and Mackenzie all revelling in a physical approach that Spurs had difficulty overcoming. Hutchinson, a mid-season acquisition from Coventry City, was to be the key man in the game. After half an hour, he stretched fully to convert Ranson's cross and give City the lead and, with the Manchester club in ascendancy, Spurs were staring defeat in the face as the match wore on. Villa, ineffective, was substituted for Garry Brooke in the second half and, as the big Argentine trudged inconsonantly towards the tunnel, it seemed to capture Tottenham's day precisely. But then, with little over ten minutes remaining, Spurs were thrown a lifeline, with Hutchinson – the oldest player on the pitch at thirty-three – again involved. Perryman laid a free-kick on the right corner of the City area back to Hoddle and the midfielder curled the ball towards the left side of the City net, which Corrigan appeared to have covered. But breaking from the defensive wall at the last second, the ball struck the moving Hutchinson and flew into the right side of the City net. It was cruel luck on City but, as Hoddle rejoiced, Spurs knew they had escaped, and when extra time brought no further goals, the team knew they had probably underestimated City and would have to improve drastically in the replay five days later.

Much of the discussion following the first game was whether Villa would retain his place in the Spurs line-up. He had performed miserably on the Saturday. But Burkinshaw was developing into a wise old head, and knew better than anyone what was right for his team. He sympathised with his player's unhappiness and knew the inconsistent Argentine was unlikely to play as badly again, and had no hesitation in picking him once more. The confidence shown in him by his manager seemed to rejuvenate Villa and, in the replay he was a totally different character – wanting the ball, and more importantly, proving effective with it.

Spurs, as they knew they had to, came out playing much better football right from the get-go, attacking Manchester City in menacing fashion early on. Ardiles – lively and cunning – took on two City defenders before hitting a slightly tame shot. However, the ball fell to the hovering Archibald and, when the Scot's shot was blocked by Corrigan, there was Villa to crack home the opener, the relief and joy exuding from his broad shoulders in the moment. Behind for the first time in the final, the goal stirred City into life, and for large chunks of the remainder of the contest they were on top. Three minutes after Villa's goal, they were level. Gow found

---

Tottenham Hotspur 3

Villa (2),

Crooks

Manchester City 2

Mackenzie,

Reeves (pen.)

TOTTENHAM HOTSPUR v. MANCHESTER CITY

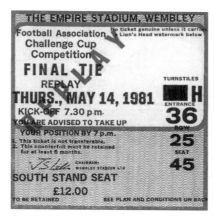

Spurs v Manchester City, replay, 1981.

Hutchinson who nodded the ball on and, from just outside the area, Mackenzie cut a perfect shape and with a lash of his right foot sent a volley that flew past Aleksic into the top left of the Spurs net. City then stunned Spurs after forty-nine minutes when a ball over the top picked out Bennett and, as he charged into the Tottenham area, he got sandwiched between Miller and Hughton and went down. Miller was adjudged to have bundled Bennett to the ground and a penalty was given. A penalty had never been missed in four previous cup final spot-kicks, and Kevin Reeves confidently kept the record intact, planting a powerful, mid-height shot to the left of Aleksic. Spurs were really up against it now, but they gradually fought their way back into the match. They were matching City physically this time, and were now starting to impose themselves as the game reached its final stages. On seventy minutes, the equaliser arrived. Hoddle chipped a ball over the top of the City defence and, as Archibald brought the ball down beautifully, Crooks nipped in from out of nowhere to blast the ball home.

The game was now on in earnest, and it was Spurs that looked the more threatening. As Galvin made a break down the left flank with just over ten minutes to play, the winger stopped, checked and played the ball back to Villa. As the big man from Argentina began his run forward, it appeared City had his run covered. But this was to be Villa's moment, the moment that forever attached itself to his football life. Twisting in and out of challenges, he danced like a giant ballerina in the City box, defenders Caton and Power left bamboozled. It seemed certain a City player would stick out a leg and clear the danger, yet Villa kept going. As Corrigan came out to block his path, Villa tucked the ball past him and into the net for what proved to be an amazing winning goal and one of the best ever witnessed at Wembley. His run had seemed to last forever yet, in reflection it happened in a heartbeat and was born of pure imagination and the desire for the unexpected, traits that perfectly belonged to Ricky Villa. The Argentine – a revelation in the replay – set off on a wild charge of celebration, and he was at least forty yards away from the scene before his teammates were able to slow him down and mob him.

The final whistle went and Spurs had won the cup. It was hard on City, as they had fully played their part in a great final, but it was Spurs that had now won six out of six FA Cup finals and, as Perryman jubilantly lifted the trophy, it signalled the beginning of a fine stretch of success in club history.

Tottenham Hotspur: Aleksic, Hughton, Miller, Roberts, Villa, Perryman, Ardiles, Archibald, Galvin, Hoddle, Crooks

Manchester City: Corrigan, Ranson, McDonald (Tueart), Reid, Gow, Caton, Power, Mackenzie, Reeves, Bennett, Hutchinson

TOTTENHAM HOTSPUR v. CHELSEA

Date: 6 March 1982

Location: Stamford Bridge

Match title: FA Cup quarter-final

Attendance: 42,557

The 1981/82 season was to be another memorable one in a very fruitful period for Spurs. Still a shade inconsistent in the league, they were improving in that respect all the time under Burkinshaw, and they were helped by a number of new additions to the squad, most notably former Liverpool goalkeeper Ray Clemence – one of the finest in his position in England – and steady centre half Paul Price who, having signed from Luton Town proceeded to get injured early in his Spurs career, but came back later in the season to command a place at the back as Spurs challenged in three cup competitions. Mike Hazard too – another gifted playmaker for the midfield, very much in the Hoddle mould – had come through the ranks and begun to earn more playing time, further emphasising Burkinshaw's desire to play attractive football.

Tottenham reached the semi-final of the European Cup Winners' Cup, beating the likes of Ajax and Eintracht Frankfurt along the way, before being kicked, quite literally, out of the competition by an uncompromising Barcelona side, 2–1 on aggregate.

The League Cup – or the Milk Cup as it had been named through sponsorship – also provided huge success for Spurs, who beat a very good Manchester United team early in the competition as they progressed all the way to the final. Spurs unfortunately suffered their first loss in a domestic cup final, although Archibald's early goal had given them a lead, which they held for a long time before going down in extra time, 3–1, to a great Liverpool side inspired by Ronnie Whelan and Ian Rush.

But it was to be the FA Cup, yet again, that would provide Spurs with further glories. The cup holders kicked-off their campaign with a tie against fierce rivals Arsenal, and Garth Crooks was to be the hero, his shot squirming through the clutches of former Tottenham great Pat Jennings to give Spurs a 1–0 win. Crooks and Mark Falco were the scorers in 1–0 home wins over Leeds United and Aston Villa respectively, setting up a mouth-watering quarter-final with Chelsea at Stamford Bridge.

At the time, Chelsea were outside the top division but, having beaten Liverpool the round before, much was expected of them, even though Spurs were favourites. The game was very exciting, yet Spurs emerged from it having played – especially in the second half – some of their best football under the Burkinshaw reign.

Chelsea were determined to give their large home crowd plenty to cheer about and came out firing, testing the Spurs back-line of Perryman, Price, Miller and Hughton, but Spurs gradually took control and set about playing some intricate, neat football. However, it was to be Chelsea that struck first. Just moments before the break, the home side went ahead when Fillery's quick free-kick caught out the Spurs wall and flew into the net.

The setback inspired Spurs and, from the outset of the second half, they clicked into overdrive, playing some wonderful football that swept Chelsea aside. The equaliser was not long coming; Hoddle's shot was spilled by the young Chelsea goalkeeper Steve Francis and arriving with predatory instincts was Archibald to sweep home Tottenham's first.

As the Spurs supporters rang out chants of 'We'll take more care of you, Archibald, Archibald', Tottenham moved forward again. A brilliant interchange of passes between Archibald and Hazard set up Hoddle who beat

Tottenham Hotspur 3	Chelsea 2
Archibald, Hoddle, Hazard	Fillery, Mayes

Ray Clemence cemented himself into the goalkeeper position for Spurs in the 1981/82 season.

Francis with a beautiful chip for the second, and then to complete a whirlwind fifteen minutes Hazard drove home a third from the edge of the area and Spurs led 3–1 to be on the brink of another FA Cup semi-final.

But, to their credit, Chelsea refused to give up, and when Spurs appeared to relax a little, they pounced. Alan Mayes hit an opportunistic second for the home side, ensuring the last few minutes of the game were uncomfortable for Spurs.

But Burkinshaw's side held out, and fully deserved to progress. They had outplayed Chelsea in the second half with a display of pure football; Hoddle, Ardiles and Hazard dominating the midfield, with Archibald a menace all game to the Chelsea defenders. For Spurs, the dream of retaining their FA Cup crown was very much alive.

Tottenham Hotspur: Clemence, Hughton, Miller, Price, Hazard, Perryman, Ardiles, Archibald, Galvin, Hoddle, Crooks

Chelsea: Francis, Locke, Hutchings, Nutton, Chivers, Pates, Rhoades-Brown, Bumsted, Mayes, Walker (Rofe), Fillery

TOTTENHAM HOTSPUR v. LIVERPOOL

Date: 13 March 1982

Location: Wembley Stadium

Match title: League Cup final

Attendance: 100,000

In the seven matches that Spurs had played in their run to the League (Milk) Cup final, they had not conceded a single goal. Now they faced the acid test in terms of the progress they had made as a side over the previous season-and-a -half. They had to face an outstanding Liverpool team at Wembley, a team that had won five of the nine previous First Division titles and were well on course to be crowned champions this time around.

Liverpool boasted some of the finest players in the land, kept the ball extremely well, were hard to break down and had a steely determination never to be beaten instilled in them by manager Bob Paisley. The central defensive partnership of Alan Hansen and Mark Lawrenson was the best in the division, they had a dynamic central midfielder in Graeme Souness – once with Spurs as a youngster – an attacking genius in Scot Kenny Dalglish and the game's most promising young striker in Ian Rush.

Liverpool were favourites and rightly so, but it was Spurs that took the lead. Archibald, top scorer at the club the previous season, had been absent with an ankle injury since December 1981 and had only recently returned to the team and, after twelve minutes, he pounced to fire Spurs ahead.

The goal should have inspired Spurs against the best team in the land, but it actually had the opposite effect. Going into something of a conservative shell, Spurs were starved of possession by Liverpool for the majority of the game, although they (under heavy pressure at the back from the moment Archibald struck) held the Reds at bay quite majestically for most of the match.

With Mike Hazard somewhat ineffective in trying to shackle the talents of Souness, Ricky Villa replaced him on sixty-five minutes, but even this move did little to spark Spurs into life.

Then came perhaps the game's decisive moment. With just ten minutes remaining, Archibald was presented with a golden opportunity to wrap the game up. If he scored to make the game 2–0, surely the cup was Tottenham's, but Archibald failed to do so and Liverpool, having received their share of luck, fought their way back into the match.

It was cruel on Spurs; despite the fact that they had done all they could to thwart the favourites, with only two minutes to go, Liverpool began an attack down the Spurs left where the ball came to substitute Craig Johnston. From an awkward position, Johnston crossed into the box and there was Republic Of Ireland Under-21 international Ronnie Whelan to equalise.

Spurs held out for the remaining moments but the goal had broken them. In the minutes of rest before extra time, Paisley could be seen rousing his players who he did not allow to sit down, giving the impression they had reserves of energy that Spurs did not. This was probably more psychological than realistic, yet a glance over to the Tottenham squad saw many of the players sprawled out on the turf or sitting down receiving treatment.

Spurs had given a brave account of themselves in the final, but it was quite clear which team was more ready for another thirty minutes of football, and so it proved. It took until twenty minutes into the extra period but Liverpool inevitably got their goal, with Whelan again the scorer, although there was some suspicion of offside, and the final nail was ruthlessly driven into the Tottenham coffin when Rush snared the third.

Tottenham Hotspur 1

Archibald

Liverpool 3

Whelan (2),

Rush

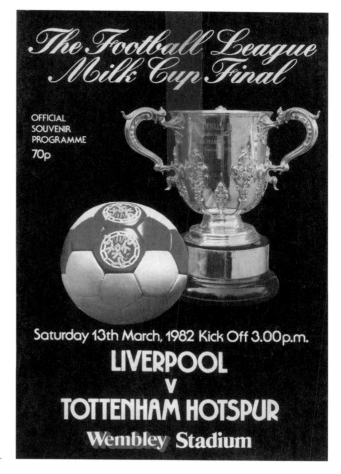

Spurs v. Liverpool, 1982.

Spurs had fought courageously for a long time but had ultimately succumbed to Liverpool, for which there was nothing to be ashamed of. The result meant Spurs had lost a major domestic cup final for the first time, but they would soon have the chance to put matters right in the FA Cup.

Tottenham Hotspur: Clemence, Hughton, Miller, Price, Hazard (Villa), Perryman, Ardiles, Archibald, Galvin, Hoddle, Crooks

Liverpool: Grobbelaar, Neal, Lawrenson, Kennedy, Thompson, Whelan, Dalglish, Lee, Rush, McDermott (Johnston), Souness

TOTTENHAM HOTSPUR v. QUEENS PARK RANGERS

Date: 27 May 1982

Location: Wembley Stadium

Match title: FA Cup final replay

Attendance: 92,000

When it came time to play in the 1982 FA Cup final (having beaten Second Division Leicester City 2–0 in the semi-final), Spurs had already played an incredible 63 games in their season. They had experienced a deep run in the European Cup Winners' Cup, reached the final of the League Cup and maintained a high position in the First Division. That they eventually managed to finish fourth in the league was a testament to how far the club had progressed under Burkinshaw for, after the FA Cup semi-final against Leicester at the beginning of April, Spurs had to make up an extraordinary number of games due to their cup exploits, often playing three, sometimes four, games a week until the end of the season, with injuries becoming increasingly frequent.

But Spurs held firm, finishing fourth in the league and, although they may have been extremely jaded, they came into the FA Cup final against Second Division Queens Park Rangers as clear favourites. Missing from the Spurs side that had edged Manchester City the year before were the Argentine pair of Ardiles and Villa. The reason was the outbreak of the Falklands War between the United Kingdom and Argentina. Ardiles was stranded in Buenos Aires with his national side and could not get back, but he most likely would not have played anyway as Burkinshaw had already ruled Villa out of the final, refusing to subject his player – already a target of abuse from rival fans – to the pressures of playing in such a high-profile match at such a difficult time. With Mike Hazard a natural replacement for Ardiles in midfield, the versatile Graham Roberts moved up from defence to take his place alongside Hoddle in the centre of midfield.

Former Tottenham player and a future manager of the club Terry Venables managed QPR and their blossoming young side (that featured future Spurs players in defender Terry Fenwick and striker Clive Allen) would, in two years time, be an established First Division team themselves. Captained by a future West Ham boss, defender Glenn Roeder and featuring the talented Tony Currie in midfield, QPR had accounted for First Division West Bromwich Albion in their semi-final.

With both teams playing in change strips (QPR in red shirts and black shorts and Spurs in all yellow), the game proved a big disappointment, with Venables organising his side to frustrate and generally break up Tottenham's play rather than committing themselves to winning the game. With no goals in normal time – young QPR goalkeeper Peter Hucker having made some fine saves to deny Crooks, Hazard, Archibald and Hoddle – it was twenty minutes into the extra period that Hoddle's strike from the edge of the area took a deflection off Currie to put Spurs ahead.

But, as in the League Cup final against Liverpool, Spurs surrendered a winning lead late on. Bob Hazell flicked on Simon Stainrod's long throw and there was Fenwick, close up, to force home a header and earn QPR a replay.

QPR had frustrated Spurs and given them a hard time, and this was with Allen and later Hazell suffering injuries during the match. Hucker had undoubtedly been the star of the first game but, for the replay, they would be without their suspended captain Roeder.

Spurs again seemed below par in the replay, but they played enough good football early on to forge ahead. An inspired run by Roberts from halfway saw the powerful defender come midfielder surge into the QPR box where

Tottenham Hotspur 1
Hoddle (pen.)

Queens Park Rangers 0

TOTTENHAM HOTSPUR v. QUEENS PARK RANGERS

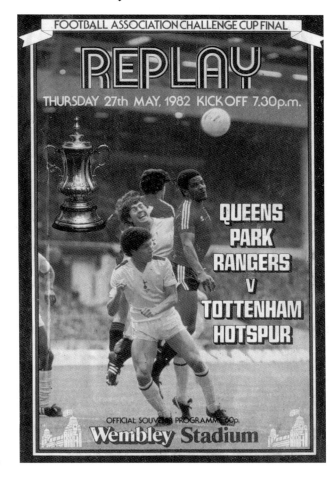

Spurs v. QPR, replay, 1982.

he was tripped by Currie. The referee had no hesitation in giving the penalty and Hoddle stepped up to drill the ball coolly past Hucker.

The goal came after only seven minutes and forced Rangers to come out and play. The Second Division side did this to the best of their ability but, despite a fair amount of pressure – coupled with the fact that Spurs played seemingly without adventure or much spirit – they could not force an equaliser.

Spurs could feel slightly downhearted that they had not played to the style associated with them but, ultimately, they had successfully retained their trophy. It had been an eventful season for Spurs, one of the busiest in their history, full of high moments, and winning the FA Cup was a fine way to end the 1981/82 campaign.

Tottenham Hotspur: Clemence, Hughton, Miller, Price, Hazard (Brooke), Perryman, Roberts, Archibald, Galvin, Hoddle, Crooks

Queens Park Rangers: Hucker, Fenwick, Gillard, Waddock, Hazell, Neill, Currie, Flanagan, Micklewhite (Burke), Stainrod, Gregory

Tottenham Hotspur v. Feyenoord

Date: 19 October 1983

Location: White Hart Lane

Match title: UEFA Cup second round 1st leg

Attendance: 35,404

The 1983/84 season was to be the last of Keith Burkinshaw's highly successful period as manager of Tottenham Hotspur. During Burkinshaw's time, the club had Sidney Wale as its majority shareholder and chairman, leaving Burkinshaw to run most aspects of the first team, such as transfer negotiations, wages and of course team selection. But when Irving Scholar worked his way into a position at the head of the board in the latter stages of Burkinshaw's reign, he made it known he favoured a Continental-style approach (ironically a system that would return to provide controversy at Spurs in future years), where the manager/head coach was only in charge of organising and picking the team. It is widely considered that Burkinshaw was not in favour of this approach and, by April 1984, it became known that he was to leave Tottenham at the conclusion of the season.

The season before, Spurs had again shown well in the league, finishing fourth behind champions Liverpool, but did not win a trophy. They did, however, start as one of the favourites for the league title in 1983/84 and with Gary Mabbutt – an emerging and versatile defender/midfielder having joined from Bristol Rovers the season before – and young defenders Danny Thomas and Gary Stevens new arrivals for the upcoming campaign, the squad had been well supplemented to complement the 'old guard' of Clemence, Hughton, Perryman, Roberts, Miller, Hazard, Hoddle, Ardiles, Galvin, Brooke, Archibald, Crooks and Falco, Villa having departed for the U.S. in the summer of 1983.

But the new season did not start well, with only one win from their first six games and, although they recovered to win five in a row from the end of September, the club would slide back into league inconsistency, although injuries at times ravaged the club. The FA Cup and League Cup competitions also failed to provide any joy for Spurs, so it was left to the UEFA Cup (they had qualified via the league the season before) as the remaining hope of sending Burkinshaw off with a trophy.

The campaign started against the Irish side Drogheda United. Spurs pulverised their opponents with a 14–0 aggregate scoreline and Mark Falco grabbed four of the goals.

Next up in the second round were the fine Dutch side Feyenoord. They were a team loaded with Dutch internationals, including two of the most famous names in world football representing two very different eras. Holding the key to the future of Dutch football was the exciting youngster Ruud Gullit, a player who would go on to win the European Championship with Holland in 1988 and also hoist multiple European Cups with AC Milan. But the most famous name in the Feyenoord side – although now in the veteran stage of his career – was Johan Cruyff, arguably the most gifted footballer of his generation. Cruyff had been at his peak in the 1970s, had enjoyed a glittering career with the likes of Ajax and Barcelona, and had played in two World Cup finals with Holland. The big attraction of this particular tie was the match up between Cruyff and the most skilful contemporary English footballer, Tottenham's very own Glenn Hoddle.

On the night, it was to be Hoddle that emerged as the undoubted king in the battle of the midfield talents, as he blatantly out-pointed both Cruyff and Gullit. Feyenoord were a very strong side, but it was Hoddle who was the creator-in-chief on this occasion, rising superbly to the challenge of Tottenham's European adventure.

Tottenham Hotspur 4
   Archibald (2),
   Galvin (2)

Feyenoord 2
   Cruyff,
   Nielsen

TOTTENHAM HOTSPUR v. FEYENOORD

Glenn Hoddle, perhaps the most naturally gifted individual ever to play for Spurs.

Hoddle created an avalanche of chances in one of the most complete halves of football that Spurs played under Burkinshaw. Two goals from Steve Archibald and two from winger Tony Galvin (who also enjoyed a marvellous game) put Spurs into an incredible 4–0 lead at half-time, and they went into the interval with unanimous applause accompanying them.

It truly was a night to remember for Spurs as they outplayed a fine side, using a quick-tempo style reminiscent of the glory days of the early 1960s. Although Feyenoord pulled two goals back in the second half, Tottenham again combined wonderfully as a team and murdered the Dutch side in the second leg, gaining a 2–0 victory with goals by Chris Hughton and Galvin to record a 6–2 aggregate victory. The UEFA Cup dream was very much alive.

Tottenham Hotspur: Clemence, Hughton, Galvin, Roberts, Stevens, Perryman, Mabbutt, Archibald, Falco, Hoddle, Brooke (Crooks)

Feyenoord: Hiele, Nielsen, Gullit, Troost, Wijnstakers, Cruyff, van Til, Hoekstra, Houtman, Jeliazkov, Duut

Tottenham Hotspur v. Anderlecht

Date: 25 May 1984

Location: White Hart Lane

Match title: UEFA Cup final 2nd leg

Attendance: 46,205

After two quite excellent performances against Feyenoord in the second round of the UEFA Cup, Spurs were drawn against German giants Bayern Munich. Featuring the likes of the great Karl-Heinz Rummennigge, Bayern had won the European Cup three times in the 1970s and, although generally considered to be a declining force at the time Spurs played them, the Germans still managed to win 1–0 in Munich. If Rummennigge's brother Michael had put away a good chance late on at White Hart Lane, it would have been the Germans and not Spurs progressing to the next round. As it was, a late winner from Mark Falco followed an early second-half goal by Archibald and Spurs were through. Austria Vienna were beaten 4–2 on aggregate to set up a tight, hard-fought semi-final with the Yugoslav side Hadjuk Split. Falco grabbed Spurs an away goal in Yugoslavia but Spurs entered the second leg 2–1 down. In a tense, guarded affair an early Mike Hazard goal put Spurs through to the final on the away goal rule.

Tottenham's opponents in the final were Anderlecht, meaning it would be the first time in the club's 39-game European history that Spurs had faced a side from Belgium. For Spurs, Hoddle was a long-term injury victim while Clemence and Ardiles were not fit enough to start the first leg, but Spurs still produced a brave performance in the match at the Constant Vanden Stock Stadium in Belgium. Falco and Gary Stevens had gone close for Spurs in the first half, while stand-in goalkeeper Tony Parks had saved well to keep out Kenneth Larsen. In the second half it looked as though it was not to be Tottenham's night when Falco missed a glorious headed opportunity, but on fifty-nine minutes, the cries of despair turned to bursts of joy. Hazard's corner was headed powerfully home from a tight angle by defender Paul Miller, giving the centre half his first goal of the season. Spurs had further chances through Falco and Graham Roberts, but the Anderlecht goalkeeper Jacques Munaron was in inspired form, virtually keeping his side in the tie, and he was rewarded for his efforts when his team snatched an equaliser with just five minutes remaining, Morten Olsen nipping in to beat Parks. It was slightly disheartening for Spurs to lose their lead late on, although not as disheartening as the booking that kept long-serving captain Steve Perryman out of the return leg at White Hart Lane.

Anderlecht had started the tie as favourites but, after Tottenham's performance in Belgium, Spurs knew that the trophy was theirs for the taking. Hoddle and Perryman were missing, while a still not fully fit Ardiles began on the bench, but this was to be a night for some of the lesser lights to shine. Mike Hazard was given the role of chief creator in midfield, while Gary Mabbutt and Gary Stevens had key roles to play in stifling what was sure to be a dangerous Anderlecht counterattacking system. Home-grown striker Mark Falco was given the chance to start his first ever major final (with the exception of the first leg in Belgium), leading the line together with Archibald and in goal was young reserve Tony Parks, again deputising for the injured Clemence and starting what was, without doubt, the biggest game of his life. In addition, Roberts captained the side in the absence of Perryman.

After an hour, Anderlecht got the goal that appeared inevitable for some time courtesy of Alex Czerniatinski, virtually silencing the vast home crowd. But the fans soon found their voices as Spurs kicked-off again, roaring their side on heroically. Unfortunately, it seemed as though Spurs could not break down the resilient Belgians,

Tottenham Hotspur 1	Anderlecht 1
Roberts	Czerniatinski
(Tottenham Hotspur won 4-3 on penalties)	

Spurs v. Anderlecht, UEFA Cup final, 1984.

who had indeed played very well. Young Scottish winger Ally Dick came on to replace Mabbutt on seventy-three minutes and then, four minutes later, Burkinshaw summoned his last throw of the dice, sending on a half-fit Ardiles in place of Miller. The latter move roused the crowd and also inspired the team as the guile and craft missing from the side was suddenly restored with the introduction of Ardiles, and the Argentine set about constructing Tottenham's attacking play. The game moved up a level as Spurs began to pressurise Anderlecht. But even Ardiles must have thought the luck was against Spurs on the night, as he burst through with time running out, only to send his shot onto the visitor's crossbar. It seemed his shot was 'the chance' and it was not to be for Spurs, but as the ball broke out to Hazard, the midfielder quickly centred the ball back in to the Anderlecht box and, appearing like a steam train, Roberts – who together with Ardiles had been the main source of Tottenham's comeback – met the cross and guided the ball past Munaron for the equaliser.

No winner was found in the remaining minutes of normal time or the half-hour of extra time, so a penalty shootout was to decide the outcome of the 1984 UEFA Cup final. Proudly striding forward to take the first kick, Roberts struck home the opening penalty. Parks then saved from Olsen to jubilant applause. Then followed a nail-biting procession of six kicks, each dispatched with authority, with Spurs scoring confidently through Falco, Stevens and Archibald, with Anderlecht netting their next three. At 4–3 to Spurs, it was a surprise to many when Danny Thomas stepped up to take the final kick for Spurs. The right-back had played very well in the final, but was not noted as a penalty taker, with many thinking Ardiles or Hazard may have been the option. But step forward bravely Thomas did to win the cup for Spurs. White Hart Lane held its collective breath, but Thomas' kick was low and smothered by Munaron. As the full-back walked back inconsolably to the centre circle, Parks steadied himself in the Spurs goal. As the blond Icelandic international Gudjohnsen took his kick, Parks threw himself to his right, pushing away the strike before setting off on a wave of emotion and glory in what was his defining career moment. Spurs had won the UEFA Cup and the team was full of heroes. It had been a wonderful period in club history under Burkinshaw, and the dramatic final was a most fitting way to send him off. The mantle was next to pass to Burkinshaw's assistant, Peter Shreeves.

Tottenham Hotspur: Parks, Thomas, Hughton, Roberts, Miller (Ardiles), Mabbutt (Dick), Hazard, Archibald, Falco, Stevens, Galvin

Anderlecht: Munaron, Hofkens, Grun, De Greef, Olsen, De Groot, Arnesen (Gudjohnsen), Vercauteren, Scifo, Czerniatinski (Brylle), Vandereycken

TOTTENHAM HOTSPUR v. WEST HAM UNITED

Date: 2 February 1987

Location: White Hart Lane

Match title: League Cup fifth round replay

Attendance: 41,995

It could be strongly argued that the last really good Spurs side to grace English football came in about 1986/87. It was the season when David Pleat had the first of his four spells as club manager, although it was the only time it was not in a caretaker capacity. Since Keith Burkinshaw's departure, Spurs had experienced a couple of up and down years under Peter Shreeves. The first year of Shreeves' reign had seen Spurs perform very well in the league, scoring a tremendous number of goals before eventually finishing third behind Everton and Liverpool. It could have been so much better as they began the New Year at the top of the table and at the beginning of March were just two points behind the leaders Everton. But after Real Madrid – featuring the experienced German sweeper Stielike, the Argentine forward Valdano and the exciting young Spanish centre forward Butragueno – ended Tottenham's hopes of retaining the UEFA Cup in the fourth round, the season came undone, and the prospect of winning the title evaporated as Spurs' form dipped. However, the following season saw Spurs slip back into infuriatingly inconsistent league form, and they could only finish tenth. The turn of fortunes cost Shreeves his job, and it was Luton Town boss Pleat that was appointed for the 1986/87 season.

From the successful side of the early 1980s, Archibald, Crooks, Hazard and Perryman had moved on in the time between Burkinshaw and Pleat (Perryman departing for Oxford United having played a club record 851 games for Spurs), and while Roberts, Miller, Galvin, Hughton and Falco remained on the fringes of the first team, it was a new batch of players that made up the core of what was to develop into a truly wonderful footballing side, albeit one destined for the most glorious of failures.

Now in the twilight of his career, Clemence remained the number one choice in goal, while Danny Thomas held the edge over Gary Stevens at right-back until Thomas cruelly suffered a career-ending injury through a tackle by QPR's Gavin Maguire in March 1987, just as he was on the verge on forcing his way into consideration for the England team. At left-back, Pleat signed the tall, rangy Mitchell Thomas from Luton Town, while to complement Mabbutt (who had moved from midfield to the centre of defence), Pleat signed the elegant but deeply commanding Richard Gough, the flame-haired Scottish international, who arrived from Dundee United and gave Spurs an outstanding pairing at the back.

The most interesting aspect of Pleat's side was the regular use of a five-man midfield. Hoddle remained the architect and was given a free role to express his talents in what would be his final season at the club before departing for Monaco. Ardiles was the schemer, while Shreeves' most exciting signing, the brilliant Chris Waddle, provided the flair, crossing ability and no shortage of spectacular goals from wide positions, although it would be in the seasons to come when he would confirm himself as one of the finest players to wear a Spurs shirt, certainly in modern times. Completing the midfield was the tireless worker Paul Allen – signed by Shreeves from West Ham – who provided bite and valuable goals, and Steve Hodge, a mid-season acquisition from Aston Villa and a player who was a midfielder of all-round ability who had represented England in the 1986 World Cup in Mexico and had a habit of making excellently timed goalscoring runs into opponents' penalty boxes from deep positions.

Tottenham Hotspur 5
Claesen, Hoddle,
C. Allen (3)

West Ham United 0

TOTTENHAM HOTSPUR v. WEST HAM UNITED

But although the Mabbutt/Gough combination was a rock-like base, the unusual midfield a stroke of genius and the style of play generally born of the Tottenham way, it was unquestionably one man who fired Tottenham to the success they enjoyed in 1986/87. Feeding enthusiastically from the service provided by the likes of Hoddle, Ardiles and Waddle was striker Clive Allen, originally purchased to replace Steve Archibald when 'Archie' had left for Barcelona before the 1984/85 season. Although the initial portion of Allen's Spurs career had been blunted somewhat by injury, he was a natural goalscorer and, in a season where he revelled in his lone striker's role (although he was sometimes partnered up front by another Pleat signing, the diminutive Belgian World Cup star Nico Claesen), Allen scored an incredible 49 goals, including 33 in the league. By early February, Spurs were already on the FA Cup trail, were well positioned in the league and faced West Ham United in a fifth round replay of the League Cup, or Littlewoods Cup as it had become known through sponsorship.

Spurs v. West Ham, 1987.

The West Ham game epitomised some of the great football Spurs played during the season. Having drawn 1–1 at Upton Park – Clive Allen unsurprisingly the scorer – Spurs really turned on the style at White Hart Lane. It was an icy Wednesday evening in north London, but Spurs really came to play on the night, delighting the big crowd that had turned up. The game was just six minutes old when Ardiles put Claesen through and the Belgian coolly chipped the out-rushing goalkeeper Phil Parkes. Hoddle in particular was in magnificent form, teasing and tormenting West Ham and keeping Spurs in control throughout. The only surprise was that it took until twenty minutes from the end for the second goal to arrive. Fittingly, it was Hoddle who scored it, bending a long-range shot past the despairing Parkes for 2–0. West Ham, downcast and unable to match Tottenham's fluent football, then received a roasting, as attack after Tottenham attack caused them serious danger, and in the final ten minutes, Clive Allen helped himself to a hat-trick and Spurs ran out emphatic 5–0 victors.

Spurs were through to a League Cup semi-final and were still very much alive on three fronts in what was, at the time, looking like a season where honours were a certainty.

Tottenham Hotspur: Clemence, D. Thomas, M. Thomas, Ardiles, Gough, Mabbutt, C. Allen, P. Allen, Waddle, Hoddle, Claesen

West Ham United: Parkes, Bonds, Parris (Hilton), Gale, Martin, Devonshire, Ward, McAvennie, Orr, Cottee, Robson

Tottenham Hotspur v. Coventry City

Date: 16 May 1987

Location: Wembley Stadium

Match title: FA Cup final

Attendance: 98,000

The 1986/87 Tottenham Hotspur side was on the cusp of greatness in March 1987. They were in the semi-final of the League Cup, were strongly challenging Everton and Liverpool for the championship and were well on the road to Wembley in the FA Cup. It seemed that this Spurs side was quite capable of sweeping all before them and pillaging all the domestic honours. But the season was to take a nasty u-turn in the League (Littlewoods) Cup semi-final against arch-rivals Arsenal. In a hostile first leg at Highbury, a Clive Allen goal saw Spurs return to White Hart Lane with the advantage, and when Allen again scored in the second leg it appeared Spurs were heading to Wembley. But when Viv Anderson and Niall Quinn scored for Arsenal, the tie went to a replay. Spurs won the coin-flip for home advantage, and Allen scored for the third game running to put Spurs in the driving seat. But with time running out Allinson equalised for Arsenal and, when Rocastle grabbed a winner with barely seconds remaining, Spurs lost in the cruellest of fashions, defeat the most bitter of pills to swallow for both players and fans alike. The defeat to Arsenal could have seriously affected team morale and performance but, to Tottenham's credit, they won their next two league games. However, with an FA Cup run in full flow, the league fixtures began to congest and, losing four of their last seven matches, Spurs had to settle for third place for the second time in three years, again behind champions Everton and second-placed Liverpool.

But in the FA Cup Spurs were very much alive. The quarter-final threw forward a potentially dangerous trip to First Division newcomers Wimbledon and their 'Crazy Gang'. But Spurs never looked in trouble and, after Waddle had given them the lead, a delightful Hoddle free-kick booked Spurs a semi-final date with Watford at Villa Park. Watford had some very talented players, but, on the morning of the game, an injury to goalkeeper Steve Sherwood meant untested stand-in Gary Plumley had to play, and the inexperienced Plumley certainly showed his nerves as Spurs raced to a 3–0 half-time lead and, with Watford never at the races, ran out 4–1 winners.

The FA Cup final of 1987 was a chance for this fine Spurs side to end their campaign with some much-deserved silverware and send arguably their finest ever player, Glenn Hoddle, off on a winning note. Their opponents were Coventry City.

Spurs were out of the traps like whippets, Waddle in breathtaking form in the first half on the right wing, and it was he who set up the opening goal after just two minutes. Teasing and tormenting Sky Blues full-back Greg Downs, he whipped over a near-post cross that Clive Allen met with a swift header and Spurs led instantly, Coventry barely able to catch breath. At that precise moment, it appeared Spurs would roll over Coventry in a one-sided affair, but that could not have been further from the truth. Dave Bennett was their catalyst, giving Tottenham's Mitchell Thomas equally as hard a time as Waddle was giving Downs and, just seven minutes after Allen's opener, a Keith Houchen flick-on left Thomas and Steve Hodge dallying in the Spurs box, and there was Bennett to race in and tap the ball past a stranded Clemence. It was a warning for Spurs and Lloyd McGrath and Micky Gynn were winning the battle in the centre of midfield, with McGrath given the job of disrupting the play of Hoddle, while the other Spurs magician, Ardiles, was virtually anonymous during the match. But Tottenham, nevertheless, continued to make chances as they had done all season, and it was Hoddle who chipped towards an empty net after a mistake by the Coventry goalkeeper Steve Ogrizovic on thirty minutes, only to be denied

Tottenham Hotspur 2	Coventry City 3
C. Allen,	Bennett, Houchen,
Mabbutt	Mabbutt (o.g.)

by a late clearance from defender Trevor Peake. Spurs had other chances in the first half and, in hindsight, that was where they should have won the match, but their only reward was a second goal that arrived after forty minutes. Hoddle's free-kick caught Ogrizovic in no man's land, and Mabbutt beat the City captain Brian Kilcline to the cross and turned the ball into the net for a 2–1 lead at half-time.

The second half began and, just as Spurs appeared set to take a stranglehold on the game, Coventry orchestrated a breakaway. Again it was Bennett who shot clear down the right and, as his cross came in, the tall forward Houchen met the ball at full stretch with a diving header to register one of the most spectacular and recognisable goals in cup final history. The longer the game went on, the more tired Spurs looked. Claesen and Stevens replaced two of the veterans, Chris Hughton and Ardiles, respectively but, as the match proceeded into extra time, it was Coventry that were finishing the stronger. Having performed admirably in generally blunting the threat of Hoddle, McGrath then set about twisting the knife

Spurs v. Coventry, FA Cup final, 1987.

in Tottenham's back. Running powerfully down the right, McGrath took a swing at the ball that appeared more like a cross, but Mabbutt's outstretched leg diverted the ball agonisingly over Clemence and into the far corner of the Spurs net. It was a terribly cruel way to lose a final, but it was to prove the winning goal. As chief coach Sillett and the Coventry players revelled in Coventry's unexpected first ever FA Cup win, the Spurs players trudged, downhearted, around the pitch. It was a shame for Hoddle not to bow out of a wonderful Spurs career on a winning note, but the real shame was that this undoubtedly high-class Spurs side won nothing in a season that had promised to reap a rich harvest of honours. No sooner had Pleat put his side together, than it broke up. Hoddle was leaving, everyone knew that, but Clemence and Ardiles were nearing the end of their great careers, while Gough – an inspirational rock since arriving from Dundee United – was soon to return to Scotland for family reasons. Clive Allen, Hodge and Claesen would only have one more season at the club and further to this, after allegations surrounding his private life, Pleat was forced to resign early in the next season.

Then began the Terry Venables era at White Hart Lane, as the new boss set about the task of building another new side for the club he had once served as a player.

Tottenham Hotspur: Clemence, Hughton (Claesen), M. Thomas, Hodge, Gough, Mabbutt, C. Allen, P. Allen, Waddle, Hoddle, Ardiles (Stevens)

Coventry City: Orgrizovic, Phillips, Downs, McGrath, Kilcline (Rodger), Peake, Bennett, Gynn, Regis, Houchen, Pickering

Tottenham Hotspur v. Arsenal

Date: 14 April 1991

Location: Wembley Stadium

Match title: FA Cup semi-final

Attendance: 77,893

Terry Venables was already a highly touted and heavily respected manager when he arrived at Spurs. He began his managerial career at Crystal Palace and enjoyed great success, guiding the Eagles from the Third Division to the First, and he was then in charge of the Queens Park Rangers side that gave Spurs such a hard time in the 1982 FA Cup final. Having had success on the domestic scene with a pair of smaller clubs, Venables' next stop could not have been more of a contrast, as he took charge of Barcelona, where one of his first signings was Tottenham's Steve Archibald. Venables achieved some success at the Catalan club, winning the Spanish League title and reaching the final of the European Cup before going down to Romanian side Steaua Bucharest.

Having taken over from Pleat, Venables' initial season in charge brought with it dreadful results in the league as well as futile success in the cups. The summer before the 1988/89 season saw Venables attract big-money signings in forward Paul Stewart from Manchester City and a man who would prove himself a Tottenham (and England) legend in the immensely gifted, ball-dribbling, free-kick-taking, larger-than-life personality midfielder Paul Gascoigne, a £2 million purchase from Newcastle United. Although Gascoigne's Spurs career would end in despair, his three seasons at the club saw him rise from promising youngster to the most significant talent in English football in the modern era, and Spurs fans saw the very best of Gascoigne in what would be a roller-coaster footballing career, and life, for the Geordie. As well as a magnificent talent, Gascoigne was also a robust, entertaining, naïve, reckless and charming character all rolled into one stocky but supremely strong frame. In Venables, he had the ideal manager to guide him, and the man-management skills of his manager gave Gascoigne the platform to become the most wanted and most watchable performer of his time.

Nevertheless, despite Gascoigne adjusting well to life in the capital, Stewart struggled, not scoring until the tenth game of the season. Spurs won only one of those first ten games but, inspired by the incredible goalscoring form of Waddle (at his absolute peak during the 1988/89 season), and new captain Gary Mabbutt (replacing the departed Richard Gough in that capacity), with help from further Venables signings in defender Terry Fenwick, midfield craftsman Nayim and striker Paul Walsh, as well as increased playing time for home-grown midfielders Vinny Samways and David Howells, Spurs enjoyed a strong second half to the season, rising fast to finish sixth.

Waddle had scored 14 league goals and when Venables persuaded England's top striker in Gary Lineker to join from Barcelona for the 1989/90 season, Spurs suddenly stood out as genuine title contenders. But all was not well. Spurs fans were left stunned when Waddle was sold to Marseille for £4.25 million in the summer and the team again started slowly before Gascoigne, Lineker and Mabbutt pushed the side on over the closing months: Spurs won eight of their last ten to finish a highly respectable third.

Worryingly, no signings were made before the 1990/91 season and it was soon revealed that Spurs were bankrupt. When it emerged that Spurs were in serious trouble financially, uncertainty over their futures at the club appeared to affect the players on the pitch and, by the beginning of their FA Cup campaign, they were out of league title contention, looked like a club in crisis and desperately needed a major boost both financially and for the increasingly demoralised supporters.

Tottenham Hotspur 3	Arsenal 1
Gascoigne,	Smith
Lineker (2)	

Spurs v. Arsenal, FA Cup semi-final, 1991.

Tottenham Hotspur: Thorsvedt, Edinburgh, Van den Hauwe, Sedgley, Howells, Mabbutt, Stewart, Gascoigne (Nayim), Samways (Walsh), Lineker, P. Allen

Arsenal: Seaman, Dixon, Winterburn, Thomas, Bould, Adams, Campbell, Davis, Smith, Merson, Limpar (Groves)

TOTTENHAM HOTSPUR v. ARSENAL

As it so often had for Tottenham Hotspur, it was to be the FA Cup that provided the spark and breathed life into the season. Paul Stewart, now playing an attacking central-midfield role, scored the winner against his former club Blackpool in the third round, while the next three rounds saw Gascoigne almost carry Spurs through by himself. The midfielder was in truly dominant form (despite being bothered constantly by injury), scoring twice in the 4–2 home win against Oxford United, two more at Portsmouth in the fifth round, and the winner against Notts County in the quarter-final.

But crucially, Gascoigne was forced to succumb to the injury that had hampered him for some time, and he underwent a double hernia operation after the Notts County game that put a question mark against the rest of his season. If Tottenham were going to reach another cup final, surely they would need their most gifted player? This fact became even more obvious when they were drawn against Arsenal in the semi-final, with the match the first of its kind to be played at Wembley.

Although Gascoigne and fellow midfielder Howells had missed significant time through injury before the Arsenal match, both were selected in a match-day gamble by Venables against a side that was destined to win the First Division title and thus was gunning for the 'double'. Arsenal were managed by George Graham and, with a rock-solid defence supporting a dangerous attack, started the game as heavy favourites. For Spurs, the inspirational captain Mabbutt and feisty midfielder Paul Allen survived from Tottenham's 1987 FA Cup final team. The tall, blond Norwegian Erik 'The Viking' Thorsvedt had cemented the goalkeeping position, despite some early troubles, since joining from Viking Stavanger, while two more Venables signings – the experienced Pat Van den Hauwe and youngster Justin Edinburgh – gave Spurs two aggressive full-backs. Midfielder-cum-centre half Steve Sedgley – prone to the occasional blunder but determined and strong nonetheless – was Mabbutt's partner at the back having been signed by Venables from Coventry City in 1989 while Samways, Stewart and Lineker completed the line-up that faced Arsenal, with another former Barcelona man, Nayim, plus Walsh, on the bench.

In the event it was a day that no Spurs fan will ever forget, and the atmosphere for the first ever Wembley semi-final was colourful, passionate, wild and unique, making it an FA Cup occasion for the ages.

Almost from the outset, it was clear that Spurs would have no part of their underdog status, as they began the game in inspired fashion. As competitive and crisp as the tackles that shocked Arsenal early on were, it was Spurs' fluent, short-passing game that gave them all the initial possession.

After just five minutes, the first thunderbolt was struck. Fully thirty yards out, Gascoigne – belying his long absence through injury – strode up and simply whacked an unstoppable free-kick into the top right-hand corner of Arsenal goalkeeper David Seaman's net. As Gascoigne set-off on a jubilant celebration, the din created by the Spurs support was thunderous.

Arsenal seemed shocked by the goal, and Spurs took advantage with ruthless effect just a few minutes later. As Gascoigne combined with Allen down the right, the latter's cross seemed to take an age to reach the box, evading Arsenal defenders as it did so but, when it arrived, Lineker slid in bravely and turned the ball home. With barely ten minutes gone, Spurs were unbelievably 2–0 up. Tottenham fans were in a frenzy. Arsenal were stunned; they had been so heavily fancied to win, but now came the true test of their resolve.

Very few north London derbies are easily won, and Arsenal began to play in the latter stages of the second half. Then, moments before the break, Arsenal broke forward through right-back Lee Dixon. As his deep cross entered the Spurs box, there was the tall striker Alan Smith to meet it, beating Mabbutt, and steering the ball past Thorsvedt for 2–1.

Spurs had exceeded expectations in the first half; Gascoigne, Howells, Samways and Allen outstanding in midfield, but all Spurs fans were bracing themselves for the expected Arsenal onslaught in the second half. After

Gascoigne (8) fires his incredible free-kick against Arsenal.

all, this was a team that would score 74 goals in their league campaign against a mere 18 conceded, while Tottenham had scored a solitary goal more than they had let in during the same time (51–50) but still, Spurs defended with enormous credit in the second half.

Led on majestically by Mabbutt, the defence held firm, knowing all the time the breakaway was on if they could spring the attack while Arsenal poured pressure on them. Gascoigne, clearly tiring, was substituted on the hour to be replaced by Nayim, and then on seventy-eight minutes the killer blow was delivered.

Samways sent Lineker through and, having outpaced the Arsenal defence, the England striker zoned in on the out-rushing Seaman. From the right side of the Arsenal box, Lineker got his shot away as Tony Adams closed with a challenge and, although Seaman was guilty of misjudging the shot and could only push it slightly to his right, Lineker's effort had enough power to find its way into the left side of the Arsenal net. That made it 3–1 Spurs, and as Lineker lay overjoyed on the turf, he was mobbed by his elated teammates.

Arsenal had a number of chances late on but Spurs would not cave. They had defied the odds and each and every player had done their bit in ensuring Tottenham would be returning to Wembley for another cup final.

Gascoigne was acclaimed the hero, but the defence, particularly Mabbutt and Sedgley, had been magnificent. The Spurs players rightly celebrated with their buoyant fans long after the final whistle in enjoying one of the most memorable games in recent Spurs history, knowing that an appearance in an FA Cup final could not have come at a more appropriate or vital time for the financially strapped club.

TOTTENHAM HOTSPUR v. NOTTINGHAM FOREST

Date: 18 May 1991

Location: Wembley Stadium

Match title: FA Cup final

Attendance: 80,000

None of their previous eight FA Cup final appearances had carried with them as much importance to Tottenham Hotspur Football Club than their ninth visit, against Nottingham Forest. Spurs were desperately in debt and in dire need of a boost both financially and for morale. A deal worth over £8 million had been agreed to take the club's prized asset, Gascoigne, to the Italian club Lazio at the end of the season, therefore the cup final was to be the Geordie's last ever appearance for Spurs. Whether Tottenham could achieve that success was debatable, and opinion was divided before the match as to who were the favourites. Legendary manager Brian Clough had developed – as usual – a good footballing side featuring England stars in left-back Stuart Pearce, centre-back Des Walker and forward Nigel Clough, while in the heart of their midfield was young Irishman Roy Keane, an emerging talent of unlimited potential. It was common knowledge that the FA Cup – the one trophy to elude him as both player and manager – was the competition Clough now most dearly wanted to win as he entered the twilight of a managerial career, and thus public sentiment favoured Forest.

However, it soon became clear that Gascoigne was in an intense, wired-up mood as he set out to mark his last Spurs game in style. An eccentric character at the quietest of times, Gascoigne went in on Forest midfielder Garry Parker with a boot to the chest for which he was lucky not to have been dismissed instantly. Worse was to follow as Forest enjoyed the bulk of the early possession; what happened next will be remembered by Spurs fans as much as his wonderful strike against Arsenal in the semi-final. Scything down Forest's advancing right-back Gary Charles on the edge of the Spurs area, Gascoigne's reckless challenge left both players on the ground. It was a foul to be ashamed of, and probably worthy of a red card given the earlier foul on Parker but, as Charles eventually clambered to his feet, it was becoming clear that Gascoigne was seriously hurt. Rising most gingerly, Gascoigne could only watch in anguish as Pearce blasted an unstoppable free-kick into the Spurs net. As Forest rejoiced, Gascoigne crumpled to the floor in pain. His cup final was over, he had suffered serious cruciate ligament damage, and it later emerged his career too now hung in the balance. The loss of Gascoigne was a body blow to Spurs. He had scored six goals as the chief inspiration on the road to Wembley and it would not have surprised many if Spurs had folded with the loss of their star player so early. But Nayim came on; Spurs regrouped and gradually began to get on top of Forest. Lineker had a strike midway through the first half ruled out for offside, but replays proved the goal should have counted and then, late in the half, the Forest goalkeeper Crossley tripped Lineker in the area giving Spurs a penalty. In a first half that had drained the emotion of every Tottenham supporter, Lineker saw his spot kick well saved by Crossley.

On fifty-five minutes, Spurs got their deserved equaliser. Paul Allen and Nayim interchanged passes before releasing Stewart. Attacking the right-hand side of the Forest box, Stewart shot low and hard through a gang of Forest defenders, and his accurately drilled strike beat Crossley to the goalkeeper's right and nestled in the far corner of the net.

As the game progressed into extra time, Spurs were clearly the stronger and, in the early stages of the first extra period, they forced a corner. Nayim took it and Stewart flicked the ball on towards the far post. There, steaming

---

Tottenham Hotspur 2
  Stewart,
  Walker (o.g.)

Nottingham Forest 1
  Pearce

TOTTENHAM HOTSPUR v. NOTTINGHAM FOREST

Spurs v. Nottingham Forest, FA Cup final, 1991.

in and wearing the captain's armband was Mabbutt, and as he lunged to head goalwards, Forest defender Walker stuck his head out and diverted the ball in for an own goal. It was fitting that it should be Mabbutt that caused the goal, for he had been forced to live with his unfortunate own goal against Coventry in the 1987 final and, although tough on Walker, it proved to be the winning goal. Spurs had won the cup for an eighth time and nobody wore a bigger smile than Gary Mabbutt as he thrust the cup aloft after leading his Spurs teammates up the famous Wembley steps to collect their prize. Sympathy went out to Clough and, although he had caused his own downfall, it was impossible not to feel sorry for Gascoigne. In the event, Gascoigne's transfer was put on hold, but it later went through, although at a cost of some £3 million to Spurs, who were forced to accept a reduced transfer fee. Meanwhile, a combination of Venables and leading businessman Alan Sugar took hold of the club and eventually sorted out the huge financial mess. Former boss Peter Shreeves took charge of the first team the following season as Sugar became chairman and Venables chief executive.

But unfortunately for Spurs, results suffered for the next few seasons as first Shreeves and then a combination of Doug Livermore and Ray Clemence failed to achieve any sort of success. All the while, Venables oversaw first-team affairs, signing players of the calibre of subsequent England internationals in winger Darren Anderton and striker Teddy Sheringham as well as introducing another future England star, attacking midfielder Nick Barmby, to the first team. But having finished eighth at the end of the 1992/93 season, Venables was sacked, sparking a long legal battle with Sugar that the chairman eventually won. Although there had been many disappointing and unfulfilling moments in his time at Spurs, Venables did achieve a certain degree of success. He won the FA Cup, achieved a placing of third in the league, been beaten semi-finalists in another FA Cup run and attracted a decent number of big-name players to the club while always eager to introduce young, home-grown talent. Yet his departure left a bitter taste in the mouths of Spurs supporters and, rightly or wrongly, Sugar never recovered the support of the Tottenham fans, despite pouring huge amounts of money into the club for player purchases. The Venables era had been nothing if not interesting, and Sugar's first selection without him was to appoint Spurs legend Ossie Ardiles as manager, poaching him – literally – away from West Bromwich Albion to begin another fascinating era of Tottenham Hotspur football.

Tottenham Hotspur: Thorsvedt, Edinburgh, Van den Hauwe, Sedgley, Howells, Mabbutt, Stewart, Gascoigne (Nayim), Samways (Walsh), Lineker, P. Allen

Nottingham Forest: Crossley, Charles, Pearce, Walker, Chettle, Keane, Crosby, Parker, Clough, Glover (Laws), Woan (Hodge)

Tottenham Hotspur v. Sheffield Wednesday

Date: 20 August 1994

Location: Hillsborough

Match title: FA Premiership

Attendance: 34,051

Just three years after capturing the FA Cup, the Tottenham Hotspur side that began the 1994/95 season had a totally different look about it than the one that beat Nottingham Forest at Wembley. Ossie Ardiles' first campaign in charge the season before had proved most disappointing, fielding an inconsistent side that finished fifteenth in the second year of the newly formed FA Premiership, while experiencing no joy in the cups.

Even though former chairman Irving Scholar had long gone by the start of the 1994/95 campaign, the then-board's dealings during their time at the club – which had included making illegal payments – had been revealed and the FA decided to take strong action against Spurs. The club were fined £600,000, but even worse was the twelve-point penalty inflicted before the season had even begun, meaning an already average side would have to win four games simply in order to reach zero points, and this for a club that had won only eleven league games the season before. To add insult to injury, Spurs were banned from taking part in the season's FA Cup, a cherished competition for all associated with the club.

It was probably this particular season when chairman Alan Sugar showed his deepest commitment to the Tottenham cause. Through an appeal, the twelve-point penalty was reduced to six (even though the fine rose by £900,000) and with Spurs preparing to start the season with at best a mid-table side, Sugar – who had by now got Spurs back on a steady ship financially – provided Ardiles with a £10 million war chest to strengthen his squad. When the club signed the brilliant German World Cup striker Jurgen Klinsmann from Monaco, and then added one of the stars of Romania's exciting World Cup run in the USA, the attacking left-sided forward Ilie Dumitrescu, it was if a new lease of life had been breathed into White Hart Lane. Not long into the season, the elegant defender Gica Popescu – another high-class World Cup star with Romania – was signed, and Spurs suddenly had the basis of an exciting team. Ian Walker had come through the ranks to unseat Erik Thorsvedt in goal, and the promising centre half duo of England Under-21 stars Sol Campbell and Stuart Nethercott had broken into the side to accompany the likes of Mabbutt, Edinburgh and an Ardiles signing from Swindon Town the season before, Scotland's Colin Calderwood, in defence.

But it was the Spurs attack that really caught the eye at the start of the season. Although Popescu did not arrive until the season was underway, Klinsmann and Dumitrescu both started the first game of the season at Sheffield Wednesday and played their part in what – at least for a while – would be known as the 'famous five'. Ardiles believed he had the players to achieve all-out attacking football, and with the forward-thinking Anderton on the right, Dumitrescu on the left and Nick Barmby in a central role, the midfield certainly had a distinctly attack-minded feel to it, while up front were Sheringham (top scorer the season before) and of course the new superstar, Klinsmann, and it was the latter who very much stole the headlines on his Spurs debut.

The season began with a wonderful start for Spurs with a goal just nineteen minutes into the game. As Anderton crossed into the box there was Sheringham, unmarked and able to slot his shot calmly past Wednesday goalkeeper Kevin Pressman. Then the advantage was doubled when Sheringham turned provider and played Anderton through into the Wednesday area where he slid it past Pressman for 2–0.

Tottenham Hotspur 4

Sheringham, Anderton,
Barmby, Klinsmann

Sheffield Wednesday 3

Petrescu, Calderwood (o.g.),
Hirst

TOTTENHAM HOTSPUR v. SHEFFIELD WEDNESDAY

Ardiles' signing of Klinsmann (left) and Romanians Dumitrescu & Popescu breathed life into a demoralised Spurs club.

Two goals ahead, Spurs could have concentrated on defending their lead but, indicative of how the Ardiles reign would develop, Spurs were soon pegged back. Wednesday pulled a goal back when another Romanian, Dan Petrescu, controlled Sheridan's pass and casually beat Walker. Then they were level when, under pressure from midfielder Chris Bart-Williams, Calderwood diverted past his own goalkeeper.

Spurs continued to attack relentlessly, Dumitrescu receiving warm applause from the travelling faithful when he was replaced by the veteran Mike Hazard, who had returned to the club the season before and, with just under twenty minutes to go, Sheringham flicked on a long pass that found Barmby, whose shot from the edge of the box went through the legs of former Nottingham Forest defender Des Walker, evaded Pressman and went in.

Spurs were really turning on the style now, playing with the fluency and pace of past glory days, and the crowning moment arrived soon after as Anderton – having a fine game – picked out Klinsmann at the back post, and the unmistakable blond figure leapt high to power a header into the Wednesday net for 4–2. Klinsmann then set off on an infamous goal celebration. During his career – particularly with the German national side – Klinsmann had garnered a reputation as something of a diver and, in the days leading up to his Spurs debut, had received negative press regarding the matter. Having scored his goal, he set off for the touchline where he proceeded to 'dive' to the turf and was promptly joined with similar efforts by his delighted teammates.

Wednesday fought to the end – before which Klinsmann left the game on a stretcher following a clash of heads with Walker – and scored a third goal through a cracking David Hirst volley. But Spurs held out for a dramatic 4–3 win, and with it came the emergence of a new hero in Klinsmann.

Tottenham Hotspur: Walker, Kerslake, Edinburgh, Campbell (Mabbutt), Nethercott, Calderwood, Barmby, Dumitrescu (Hazard), Sheringham, Klinsmann, Anderton
Sheffield Wednesday: Unknown

TOTTENHAM HOTSPUR v. SOUTHAMPTON

Date: 1 March 1995

Location: The Dell

Match title: FA Cup fifth round replay

Attendance: 15,172

The arrival of Klinsmann and the Romanians, plus Ardiles' penchant for playing all-out attacking football, had made Spurs one of the most desirable teams to watch in the early stages of the 1994/95 season. But at times the attacking football employed bordered on the kamikaze, and there were some heavy league defeats early on. But the real low point came in the third round of the League Cup when Spurs were dumped out of he competition 3–0 by Notts County, a side bottom of Division One (old Second Division). The result seemed too much for Sugar to bear and, after the next league game at home to West Ham – which Spurs won 3–0 with Popescu playing as a sweeper – Ardiles was sacked.

To most, it appeared something of a panic measure, but Tottenham's defence was undeniably a huge concern. They had conceded 24 goals through the first twelve league games, a further 9 in three League Cup games (against lower league sides Watford and Notts County) and with the exception of the West Ham game, had failed to keep a single clean sheet. The man Sugar turned to was QPR manager Gerry Francis, not known for his flair and adventure but rivalled by few for his organisational skills. Francis elected to play with a tight 4-4-2 formation, recalling David Howells to the centre of midfield alongside Popescu and dropping the crowd favourite but defensively inept Dumitrescu. Despite losing a crazy game, 4–3, to Aston Villa on his Spurs managerial debut, Francis quickly got the sinking Spurs ship in order, and stabilised them to the point where they went unbeaten in the next ten games.

Better was to come in what was becoming a wild season for the club. Sugar had worked overtime to pressurise the powers that be into reversing their decision to ban Spurs from the FA Cup, and eventually there came the news that the six points they had been penalised had been wiped clear and Spurs were reinstated in the cup.

Spurs then set off on a memorable FA Cup run. After beating non-league Altrincham 3–0 at home in the third round, Spurs won 4–1 at Sunderland a round later. Next came a date with Southampton – a side featuring a seriously in-form Matthew Le Tissier – at White Hart Lane, and despite a Klinsmann goal, Spurs were forced into a replay at The Dell.

It was one of the most memorable games in recent Spurs history just for the sheer turnaround from the first half to the second. The Dell had never been an easy place for visiting teams to go and the unique atmosphere of the small, compact ground seemed likely to doom Spurs to a fifth round exit after one half of football. The Saints had taken a quick lead when Neil Shipperley had scored and when Le Tissier stroked home a penalty five minutes before half-time, Spurs looked dead and buried.

But this game was destined to be remembered for one man; Spurs forward Ronny Rosenthal, on as a substitute just prior to half-time for Stuart Nethercott. Rosenthal had been a signing of Ardiles' from Liverpool, with both his spell at the Anfield club and at White Hart Lane mediocre at best. Rosenthal was often looked at as a figure of fun by the fans at White Hart Lane, his bustling, head-down, straight-line running down the flanks so often ending in him falling over or meeting a dead end. But on this March evening, he delivered the performance of a lifetime.

Tottenham Hotspur 6	Southampton 2
Rosenthal (3), Barmby,	Shipperley,
Sheringham, Anderton	Le Tissier (pen.)

Tottenham Hotspur v. Southampton

Spurs v. Southampton, 1995.

Two breathtaking strikes in two minutes flew past the Southampton goalkeeper Bruce Grobbelaar, and Spurs were level in the blink of an eye. With the game going into extra time, it was Rosenthal who completed a most stunning hat-trick to put Spurs ahead, and as he did so, Southampton deflated.

Incredibly, Barmby, Sheringham and Anderton added further goals as Spurs ran out emphatic 6–2 winners. Unfortunately, Rosenthal never enjoyed such a night again, but his three goals will forever be remembered at Tottenham, and because of Ronny Rosenthal, Spurs secured a place in the last eight of the FA Cup.

Tottenham Hotspur: Walker, Edinburgh, Calderwood, Austin, Mabbutt, Nethercott (Rosenthal), Anderton, Barmby, Howells (Caskey), Sheringham, Klinsmann

Southampton: Grobbelaar, Dodd, Monkou, Benali, Kenna, Widdrington (Hughes), Magilton, Maddison, Heaney, Le Tissier, Shipperley

Tottenham Hotspur v. Liverpool

Date: 11 March 1995

Location: Anfield

Match title: FA Cup quarter-final

Attendance: 39,582

Just ten days after their dramatic revival against Southampton at The Dell, Spurs were back in pursuit of FA Cup glory in a season that had begun with the near-certain prospect of winning absolutely nothing. In their quarter-final match, Spurs were handed a most difficult tie with a trip to Anfield to face Liverpool.

Liverpool, although nowhere near the force they were in the 1980s, were still one of the top sides in the Premiership (they eventually finished fourth with Spurs seventh) and could boast some exciting talent in past, present and future England internationals in goalkeeper David James, midfielder Jamie Redknapp (who would play for Spurs later in his career), attacking wingers John Barnes and Steve McManaman and young striker Robbie Fowler, as well as former Spurs defender Neil 'Razor' Ruddock.

For Spurs, the hero from the Southampton game, Israeli Ronny Rosenthal, kept his place to face his former team but, despite Tottenham's positive change of fortunes under Gerry Francis, Liverpool started the game as firm favourites.

Spurs came into the game on the back of a 3–0 home win against Ipswich Town in the league, but it was Liverpool that dominated much of the first half. With Fowler in fine form, the young marksman gave the home side the lead on thirty-eight minutes. The home crowd may well have expected their team to push on from there and swamp Tottenham, but it was to be the Spurs fans that were the next to celebrate.

Moments before half-time, the ball found its way to Sheringham in a dangerous position and he proceeded to bend a shot accurately past James, sending the Spurs fans wild. The goal had arrived at a perfect time for Tottenham; they had survived the most dangerous spells that Liverpool would conjure, and in the second half Spurs looked very comfortable. But after Sheringham's late goal in the first half, a far more dramatic twist lay in wait as the game approached full time.

With both sides having apparently settled for a draw, Spurs ventured forward with just a minute to play. All season long, the Sheringham-Klinsmann partnership had worked beautifully, and now it would be seen at its deadliest, epitomising the understanding the two had created as a tandem. Playing a one-two with Sheringham, Klinsmann suddenly found himself surging into the Liverpool box. Instinctively striking a firm shot past James, the ball rippled the back of the net to give Spurs a most memorable win against the odds at Anfield to reach the semi-finals of the FA Cup.

It was a truly dramatic end to the match, but Spurs had shown resolve, calmness and clinical finishing to progress. The Liverpool supporters, seeing their team knocked out of the competition, generously and sportingly applauded the Spurs players – particularly Klinsmann – off the pitch.

The FA Cup dream however, would end in the next round for Spurs, as they found the blue team from Merseyside a different proposition altogether at Elland Road, Leeds. Spurs were favourites on the day as the

Tottenham Hotspur 2	Liverpool 1
Sheringham,	Fowler
Klinsmann	

A view from inside modern-day White Hart Lane.

prospect of a Tottenham Hotspur *v.* Manchester United cup final loomed large, but it was Everton that totally outplayed Spurs and, inspired by Nigerian Daniel Amokachi, they ran out 4–1 winners as Tottenham never hit their stride. In the event, Spurs lost to the eventual cup winners, as Everton went on to beat Manchester United 1–0 in the final with a winning goal scored by striker Paul Rideout.

Tottenham Hotspur: Walker, Edinburgh, Calderwood, Austin, Mabbutt, Rosenthal, Anderton, Barmby, Howells, Sheringham, Klinsmann

Liverpool: Unknown

TOTTENHAM HOTSPUR v. WIMBLEDON

Date: 2 May 1998

Location: Selhurst Park

Match title: FA Premiership

Attendance: 25,820

The Gerry Francis era never captured the imaginations of the Tottenham fans. After taking over and subsequently stabilising a lopsided team in the 1994/95 season and steering them to seventh in the Premiership and to the semi-finals of the FA Cup, hopes were high that Francis could take the club even further. But they slipped a place in the league the following season and fell further to tenth in 1996/97, finding no joy in the cups in either campaign – a 6–1 defeat at Bolton Wanderers in the fourth round of the 1996/97 League Cup being one of the very low points of the Francis reign.

But Francis certainly tried his best to bring glory back to White Hart Lane, for he spent a huge amount of money in the transfer market in attempting to develop the club into a Premiership force. He was not helped when Klinsmann (much to Sugar's disdain), Popescu and Barmby all left after his first season in charge, but over the next few seasons Francis recruited, at heavy cost, the likes of centre forward Chris Armstrong from Crystal Palace, wingers Ruel Fox and Andy Sinton from Newcastle United and Sheffield Wednesday respectively, much-coveted Norwegian striker Steffen Iversen from Rosenborg in Norway, Swiss centre half Ramon Vega from Cagliari in Italy, England international defender John Scales from Liverpool, Danish midfielder Allan Nielsen from Brondby in Denmark, England centre forward Les Ferdinand (for a then-club-record £6 million), and perhaps most significantly, left-winger David Ginola, the flamboyant, dazzling talent who would become arguably Tottenham's last great hero among the supporters (young striker Jermain Defoe a possible exception among the current squad). Both Ferdinand and Ginola arrived from Newcastle. Of these major signings, only Fox and Armstrong failed to represent their country at full international level.

For one reason or another, Francis never (with some sporadic exceptions) received a significant return from the majority of players he had spent Sugar's millions on. Armstrong was outstanding alongside Sheringham in his first season, scoring 21 goals in all competitions, but was dreadfully unlucky with injuries for the remainder of his Spurs career. The injury bug that seemed to curse Francis' reign with such turbulence also meant the likes of Scales, Iversen and Ferdinand could never deliver their best at Spurs, so regularly were they in the treatment room. Fox, Sinton and Nielsen were steady but unspectacular players, occasionally praiseworthy (Nielsen indeed would score a winning goal in a League Cup final for Spurs) but too frequently uninspiring, while Vega was prone to clumsy mistakes, despite his wholehearted desire to prove a success at the club, and was never the rock fans hoped would prove a worthy successor to Mabbutt at the back. So it was true that Francis was unlucky, but in his fourth season in control, the results really began to turn sour. Thirteen games into the Premiership campaign and Spurs were already out of the League Cup and faced a difficult November away game at Liverpool in the league. Despite a huge army of travelling fans, Spurs were embarrassed on the day, crushed 4–0 as the cries for Francis' head began to make themselves heard. So it was to be and soon after that game Francis resigned. Into his place stepped the virtually unknown Swiss manager of Grasshopper Zurich, Christian Gross. The new boss – somewhat bizarrely – arrived at White Hart Lane by tube for his first press conference, and quickly announced his plans to make Spurs a great force again. He proclaimed himself to be just like the fans. He enthused that

---

Tottenham Hotspur 6

Ferdinand, Klinsmann (4),
Saib

Wimbledon 2

Fear (2)

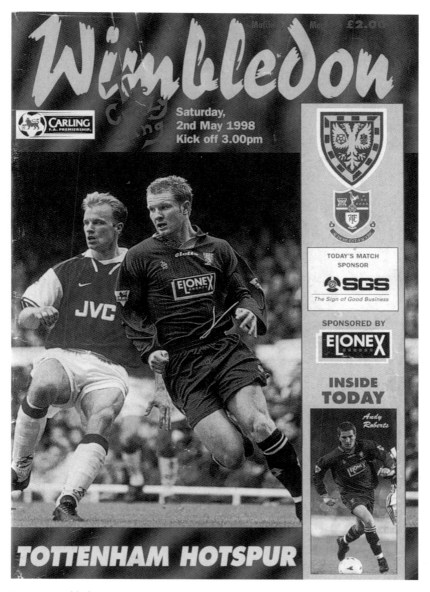

Spurs v. Wimbledon, 1998.

Tottenham Hotspur: Walker, Calderwood, Fox, Nielsen, Anderton, Ferdinand, Carr, Ginola, Campbell, Klinsmann, Berti (Saib)

Wimbledon: Sullivan, Kimble, Thatcher, Perry, McAllister, Roberts, M. Hughes, Euell, Fear, Leaburn, Kennedy

TOTTENHAM HOTSPUR v. WIMBLEDON

Ferdinand would be turned into the second coming of Harry Hotspur. What followed was a season that almost ended in relegation.

Despite Ginola beginning to display the sparkling form that would see him crowned English football's Player of the Year the following season, Spurs struggled mightily, looking at times like a desperate side heading for the drop. A fine win at Crystal Palace in late March looked sure to spark an upturn in fortune but when Spurs failed to win any of their next four games, it meant an away win at typically difficult Wimbledon was needed to be sure of entering the season's final league game assured of their safety. It was an awful proposition for such a traditionally powerful club, but it was a challenge that had to be met head on, and it is fair to say that – even though the game was played at Wimbledon's adopted home ground of Selhurst Park – a large part of the 25,000 crowd desperately craved a Tottenham win, and the support given to Spurs in such a critical, needy time was tremendous.

With all the emotion that had gone into the season, it had almost gone unnoticed when Jurgen Klinsmann had returned for a second spell at the club around Christmas time. The German had been reconciled with Sugar, and had joined to help boost Tottenham's relegation fight. Even though he had, in effect, walked out on the club after just one season to join Bayern Munich, he was greeted in the style of a true White Hart Lane legend on his return, although he was a pale shadow of the player from his first stint at the club. But Klinsmann – who also helped persuade the experienced Italian midfielder Nicola Berti to come to White Hart Lane – still had the ability to impact a game and, in the match against Wimbledon, he perhaps did more to help Spurs than in any game he had played in previously at the club. Klinsmann's second spell at the club was always intended to be temporary, and a rumoured falling out with Gross did little to help reverse this fact but, against Wimbledon, he was at his very best.

Ginola began the game in eye-catching form, hitting a Wimbledon post early on and soon after Anderton crossed for Ferdinand to bundle the ball past goalkeeper Neil Sullivan (one of three Wimbledon players – together with defenders Chris Perry and Ben Thatcher – who would eventually sign for Spurs) and put Spurs 1–0 up. It had been a hugely disappointing season for Ferdinand, from whom much was expected after his £6 million move from Newcastle, and the goal was just his fourth in the league campaign.

With Spurs in the lead after eighteen minutes and playing well, it was hard to imagine Wimbledon causing too many problems, yet by the thirty-minute mark, the home side were unbelievably 2–1 ahead following two wonder strikes from the blond-haired midfielder Peter Fear, the first a brutal thirty-yard bullet that Walker could not do anything about, the second a pile-driver from much closer in.

It could have been the signal for Tottenham to collapse; Gross staring warily on the touchline, but Spurs reacted quickly and began to play more adventurous, attacking football, striving for an equaliser. Just before half-time it arrived, as Ginola took his turn to deliver a cross into the box and there was Klinsmann to tap home.

The whole complex of the game changed early in the second half when Thatcher was sent off for a disgraceful foul on Allan Nielsen. As the Spurs player – acting as a makeshift left-back – went for a loose ball, Thatcher cut him in two with a vicious tackle that left Nielsen lucky to escape without serious injury. Understandably, the Spurs players were furious and, for a moment, an all-out brawl looked extremely likely.

With Thatcher dismissed, Wimbledon dramatically lost their shape and composure, and now it was Klinsmann's turn to shine. As Berti blocked an attempted clearance by Wimbledon's Brian McAllister, the ball fell kindly to the Italian who simply squared to Klinsmann to stroke the ball past Sullivan, and Spurs were back in front after fifty-five minutes.

Gerry Francis signed Les Ferdinand for a then-club-record £6 million.

Three minutes later, a goal kick by Walker was met by the head of Ferdinand, setting Klinsmann clean through, and the German made no mistake, recording his hat-trick and Tottenham's fourth. Spurs were now in full flow and, every time they attacked, a goal seemed likely. Two minutes later Klinsmann crowned his finest individual effort in a Spurs shirt by smacking a savage shot into the top of the Wimbledon net.

The Spurs fans were elated; their hero of past years had returned to deliver a life-saving performance to help secure the club's Premiership status. Relaxed and happy, the fans could enjoy the remainder of the game and were treated to one last goal from Algerian substitute Moussa Saib – a recent acquisition by Gross – that ended the scoring at 6–2 and finally brought to an end the threat of relegation that had haunted the club in what had been a most stressful season.

TOTTENHAM HOTSPUR v. BARNSLEY

Date: 16 March 1999

Location: Oakwell

Match title: FA Cup quarter-final

Attendance: 18,793

After the struggles of the previous season what all Spurs fans hoped for was a worry-free campaign in 1998/99, with the hope that the club could push for honours in one of the cups and also stabilise themselves with a loftier position in the Premiership; goals well attainable given the squad, although it was generally agreed that the defence and central-midfield areas needed attention in the transfer market. It would prove, ultimately, to be a successful season for Spurs, but sadly it meant that in order to achieve that success, another change of manager was necessary. When Gross had joined the club the season before, he was generally considered to be a manager who had entered a turbulent situation and may – as cruel as it may sound – not have been a big enough 'name' to handle such a job. It is true that he played his part in helping to stave off the threat of relegation and this, at least, was something to build on. But with his English never totally comprehensible and an apparent gulf between himself and many of the first-team squad, the situation always appeared on the rocks, and when Spurs failed to sign any player of note, many began to wonder if Gross could ever become the man to lead a club of the stature of Tottenham Hotspur. In fact, the only player to join the club in the summer was the virtually unknown Italian left-back Paolo Tramezzani. When Spurs lost their first two games of the season in utterly miserable fashion, Sugar acted decisively and, despite a 1–0 away win at Everton, Gross left the club as if he had never existed at White Hart Lane, and was not heard from again until a few years later when he returned to England to face Liverpool in a European competition as manager of Swiss side Basle.

Determined not to look foolish once more, Sugar began the search for a proven winner to lead Spurs forward, a sure-fire success who would command the respect of the players that Gross blatantly did not. The man Sugar turned to was former Arsenal boss George Graham. It was a controversial move and, with his Arsenal connections, it was not altogether popular. Some thought Graham simply wanted the move to be closer to London, some thought he believed Spurs to have more potential than Leeds, some darker sceptics opined that Graham's decision to join Spurs was merely to get back at former employers Arsenal, who had sacked him when it was revealed he had personally accepted a cash sum as part of the deal that had taken Danish midfielder John Jensen to Highbury in Graham's time as boss there.

The league season again developed into a disappointing hit-and-miss affair, but the cups sparked a rich vein of form that saw two memorable adventures for Spurs and their fans. Tottenham had already reached the final of the League (Worthington) Cup when they came to play at Barnsley in the quarter-final of the FA Cup. Graham had done well to shore up a leaky Spurs defence and had tightened the midfield while still embracing the talents of David Ginola, whose flair and skill was seen at its absolute best during the season. Graham signed the tall, all-round midfielder Tim Sherwood from Blackburn Rovers and also the tough-tackling German international midfielder Steffen Freund, and these two solidified the weak area of central midfield. Tramezzani never played under Graham, the new manager initially recalling long-serving Justin Edinburgh at left-back before raiding Ipswich Town for the promising Argentine Mauricio Taricco.

The match with Barnsley will never be remembered as a pure feast of football, but will certainly live long in the memory when recounting the goal that won the game for Spurs. Tottenham had already seen off Watford,

Tottenham Hotspur 1	Barnsley 0
Ginola	

Wimbledon and Graham's former club, high-flying Leeds United, in the previous rounds. Leeds were beaten in a replay at White Hart Lane in a game where Ginola was simply on fire, scoring a fantastic goal having previously hit the post after taking on the entire Leeds defence, and it was to be the Frenchman's night again at Barnsley. Having been in the Premiership the season before, Barnsley were now a Division One outfit and, on the night, gave Spurs few worries. It was Sherwood who had the first chance for Tottenham, as Anderton and Carr had worked well to set him up on the right-hand side of the box. But, adjudged to have used his hand, the opening fell away. Craig Hignett burst through for the home side midway through the first half after an error by Spurs captain Sol Campbell, but the Barnsley forward's shot was well blocked by Walker. Even though the first half was an ungraceful affair, Ginola was beginning to find his rhythm. He was often accused of 'overdoing it', but when he crossed, his arrows normally found their targets, and Armstrong, Ferdinand and Vega all came close to capitalising on the Frenchman's work.

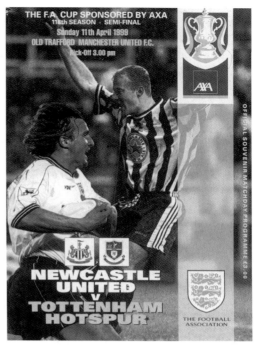

Spurs v. Newcastle United, FA Cup semi-final 1999.

It was in the second half when the game really took off. The red-haired Barnsley defender Ade Moses had been booked for obstructing Ginola – much to the annoyance of the home side – and a minute later, on the hour mark, Moses was red-carded for a late lunge on Ferdinand. Then came the goal on sixty-eight minutes that was the crowning moment for Ginola as a Spurs player. Receiving a pass from Taricco on the left touchline, Ginola began a run forty yards from goal. As the Spurs fans watched, Ginola's run seemed to be taking place in slow motion, as defender after defender was turned inside out. The closer to goal he got, the more likely he seemed to score and, having beaten five Barnsley defenders with an astonishing dribble, Ginola slid the ball along the ground to the right of goalkeeper Bullock and into the net. It was a goal of genius, a truly fantastic individual effort, ranking on a par with Ricky Villa's cup-winning goal of 1981 for pure skill (although not for importance). Ginola ripped his shirt off and headed for the celebrating Spurs supporters, with whom he was rapidly becoming a hero in the mould of Ardiles, Hoddle, Waddle and Gascoigne. It was a goal worthy of winning a cup tie, and so it proved.

For Ginola, the quarter-final had been a personal triumph, but facing his old team Newcastle United in the semi-final proved to be a brutal test, as Ruud Gullit's team marked him out of the game. In extra time at Old Trafford, Newcastle took the lead, and when a bullet drive from Alan Shearer found the top corner of Walker's net, the final nail had been driven in Tottenham's coffin, and they were out of the FA Cup.

Tottenham Hotspur: Walker, Carr, Vega, Campbell, Taricco, Anderton, Freund, Sherwood, Ginola (Sinton), Ferdinand (Iversen), Armstrong

Barnsley: T. Bullock, Moses, De Zeeuw, Morgan, Eaden, McClare (Van Der Laan), Blackmore (M. Bullock), Sinclair, Jones, Dyer, Hignett

TOTTENHAM HOTSPUR v. LEICESTER CITY

Date: 21 March 1999

Location: Wembley Stadium

Match title: League Cup final

Attendance: 77,892

The defeat in the FA Cup semi-final against Newcastle had been a blow to a Spurs side hoping to appear in the finals of both domestic cup competitions. But, three weeks before that disappointment at Old Trafford, Spurs had appeared in the League Cup final against Leicester City. It was Tottenham's first appearance in a major cup final since beating Nottingham Forest in the 1991 FA Cup final. After early round wins against lower-league sides Brentford and Northampton Town, Tottenham's road to Wembley became a difficult path laced with battles against top-flight sides. Arguably the team's best performance of the cup run came against Liverpool at Anfield in the fourth round where, dominating the game from start to finish, they ran out 3–1 winners with goals from Iversen, Scales and Nielsen. A glamour tie followed against Manchester United at White Hart Lane and, despite the Red Devils not fielding their strongest side, it proved a memorable night in north London as Armstrong scored twice and Ginola – delivering another wonderful performance – put away the third as Spurs won 3–1. In an incredible run of games, Tottenham found themselves facing London neighbours Wimbledon no fewer than five times in a period from 16 January to 16 February, and Spurs did not lose a single one of those encounters. The two clubs drew in the league, Spurs knocked the Dons out of the FA Cup at White Hart Lane in a replay after Ginola had scored to rescue a draw in the first match, and then came the two-legged semi-final in the League Cup. The first leg at White Hart Lane was tight, Spurs having the edge but being unable to break down the Wimbledon rearguard. The second leg at Selhurst Park was even closer, yet there was a strange feeling that Spurs 'had Wimbledon's number', much to the annoyance of their manager, the former Spurs player Joe Kinnear, who had not endeared himself to the Tottenham faithful through his constant belittling of Ginola's way of playing. So it proved, a beautifully executed second-half lob from Steffen Iversen being the dividing line after 180 minutes of hard-fought football. Spurs had reached the final.

It may have only been the League Cup final (the competition had taken something of a nose dive in terms of status in recent seasons with some of the higher-profile clubs fielding weakened sides) but to Spurs – in the doldrums for a few years – and a new generation of supporters, it meant the prospect of a long-awaited trophy and the mouth-watering possibility of a return to European competition. Sherwood and Taricco were cup-tied and Ferdinand was preferred to Armstrong up front, but the remainder of the team was settled and Graham had them playing well enough to be considered favourites. Of course, the match also meant the first final in English football for Ginola, and the Frenchman was obviously a key figure in the build-up to the game. For Leicester, manager Martin O'Neill had built a tough, well-organised team that were typically hard to beat. The defence was excellent with the rugged duo of Matt Elliott and Gerry Taggart leading the way, while Muzzy Izzet and Neil Lennon were central midfielders admired by a host of larger clubs. Other players of interest in the Leicester side were future Spurs goalkeeper the American Kasey Keller, the ankle-biting, blond-haired midfielder Robbie Savage, England striker Emile Heskey and the veteran centre forward Tony Cottee, a man who had enjoyed a fine career, had made his debut against Spurs as a seventeen-year-old, played for England, yet had never won a medal at Wembley Stadium, and cited this cup final as perhaps his last chance of doing so.

Tottenham Hotspur 1	Leicester City 0
Nielsen	

TOTTENHAM HOTSPUR v. LEICESTER CITY

Like the semi-final against Wimbledon, the final was a tight, hard-fought affair. No team looked dominant over the other and, for long periods, a winner was too close to call. The Leicester tactics were obvious from the outset. The Midlands side were determined to snuff out the threat posed by Ginola, and sometimes had two or three of their players hovering close to him as he tried to work his magic. Needless to say Ginola made little impact yet, conversely, Leicester offered little attacking threat themselves. The game suddenly sprang into an intense war midway through the second half. Another feature of the game was the infuriating way in which Savage had tried to wind up the Spurs midfield. Having exchanged one or two words with the equally hot-headed Freund, things got out of control. There was one laughable situation involving the two where Freund was lying on the ground kicking and lashing out at thin air hounded by angry Leicester players, but while that situation bordered on the comical, what happened next was no laughing matter for Spurs. After a challenge with Edinburgh (the only Spurs survivor from the FA Cup final team of 1991), the Spurs full-back appeared to strike out at Savage as he ran past him. Realising he had the referee's attention, Savage made the most of the

Spurs v. Leicester City, Worthington Cup final 1999.

incident and Edinburgh received a red card. Spurs were really up against it now as Leicester sensed their chance of victory. A Leicester break ended with Cottee sending the ball past the out-rushing Walker only for Vega to race back in time to clear the danger. That however, would be the closest Leicester came to scoring, and Spurs performed admirably to stay well within the game, despite the fact they must have been getting extremely tired on the large Wembley pitch. One sensed that if the game had gone into extra time then Leicester would have probably found a winner. But with normal time running out, Iversen broke down the right flank and soon found himself in the Leicester area. Directing a shot at goal, Keller parried the Norwegian's effort and surging forward from midfield was Nielsen who dived at full stretch to head into an empty net. The Spurs players celebrated ecstatically behind the goal as Leicester bemoaned their luck.

Ginola was substituted with moments to go, earning a rapturous reception as he left the pitch, proving he was the darling of the Spurs fans. It had not been his day to shine but he had played his part and, as the final whistle blew, he could celebrate with his teammates as Spurs – led by skipper Sol Campbell – walked up the famous Wembley steps to collect their first trophy for eight years, delivered to them by a manager once despised by the supporters, George Graham.

Tottenham Hotspur: Walker, Carr, Edinburgh, Freund, Vega, Campbell, Nielsen, Ginola (Sinton), Anderton, Iversen, Ferdinand

Leicester City: Keller, Ullathorne, Taggart, Elliott, Walsh, Savage (Zagorakis), Izzet, Lennon, Guppy, Cottee, Heskey

TOTTENHAM HOTSPUR v. ARSENAL

Date: 7 November 1999

Location: White Hart Lane

Match title: FA Premiership

Attendance: 36,085

The 1999/00 season promised so much but in the end delivered so little. It was to be a season of disappointment for Spurs as they failed to make a serious defence of their League Cup title, were thumped 6–1 by Newcastle in the third round of the FA Cup and, in heartbreaking fashion due to two very late goals, were eliminated by the German side Kaiserslautern in the second round of the UEFA Cup. The league form was patchy as Spurs won as many games (15) as they lost and, ultimately, a final placing of tenth was all they deserved. With the possible exception of the 7–2 home win over the Glenn Hoddle-managed Southampton (when future Spurs centre half Dean Richards scored an own goal), the highlight of the season was the home Premiership game with Arsenal, in what turned out to be one of the hottest and most fiercely contested north London derbies of modern times.

George Graham had made no glamour signings in the off-season, instead paying around £4 million for the Wimbledon centre half Chris Perry in the hope that he could develop into the long-term defensive partner for captain Sol Campbell. Norwegian midfield forager Oyvind Leonhardsen was signed on the eve of the season having fallen out of favour at Liverpool, but otherwise it was the same group as the season before.

It was the first game for Spurs after their draining loss in Germany but any questions that the players were not in the right frame of mind to meet their biggest rivals were quickly dispelled after the breathtaking start that Spurs made. The atmosphere inside White Hart Lane was electric as Spurs looked to find their first league win over Arsenal since 1995 and the play was as intense as any north London derby for many a year, as players from both sides hunted down their opponents like bloodthirsty dogs. It was Spurs that came firing out of the traps, and they sent an early warning to Arsenal when Iversen's shot was deflected for a corner. Pinning Arsenal back, Iversen raised the roof five minutes later when he scored the opening goal. Sherwood did well to block an attempted Arsenal clearance and, when the ball fell to Leonhardsen, the Norwegian picked out his countryman Iversen in the box and the tall, fair-haired striker swept the ball confidently to the left of goalkeeper David Seaman to give Spurs the lead. Spurs really found themselves in the ascendancy and, after eighteen minutes, Arsenal's French midfielder Emmanuel Petit hacked down Armstrong on the edge of the Arsenal box. After much deliberation and fussing, Spurs finally lined up to take the free-kick and, on doing so, Sherwood curled a wonderful, low shot into the opposite side of Seaman's net and Spurs led 2–0.

Not surprisingly, in a game where there were eleven yellow cards and two red ones, the tackles were flying with alarming ferocity. Arsenal began to creep back in to the game as the half wore on, and their lanky Nigerian forward Nwankwo Kanu had a goal disallowed after Armstrong had been impeded. But the visitors' pressure told on thirty-eight minutes as Petit floated over a deep free-kick. The head of the inspirational Frenchman Patrick Vieira met it and Walker could only watch as the ball hit a post and rolled over the line. The second half focused on the defending of Spurs as, led by Campbell, they produced a brilliant display under severe pressure from Arsenal. Campbell made one vital challenge to deny Ljungberg when the Swedish star ran through on goal and, from there on in, the game was ugly and ill-tempered. It was Ljungberg who very nearly sparked a free-for-all soon after. Following a scuffle with Edinburgh, Ljungberg shoved the Spurs defender to the floor and had to be

Tottenham Hotspur 2	Arsenal 1
Iversen,	Vieira
Sherwood	

Spurs v. Arsenal, 1999.

restrained further by his teammates. Referee David Elleray had little hesitation in sending off the Arsenal midfielder for violent conduct, and with the clearly angered Ljungberg's departure seemed to disappear Arsenal's hopes of forcing an equaliser. The game remained on a knife-edge however; both in terms of players' tempers boiling over and with the fact that Arsenal continued to pose an attacking threat to Spurs. Walker was forced into pulling off a fantastic double save from Dutch winger Marc Overmars and Croatian substitute Davor Suker with fifteen minutes to play, but Spurs were not to be denied, and their fans willed them home as the seconds ticked away.

Towards the end of the game, Arsenal were reduced to nine men after Keown received his second yellow card for a wild lunge on the diminutive Spurs winger Jose Dominguez – on as a late substitute for Ginola – and as the final whistle went, Spurs players and fans could rejoice in the ecstasy that only comes with beating an arch rival. George Graham had beaten his old club and, in a season of general disappointment, the highly charged north London derby win was indeed a moment to be richly enjoyed.

Tottenham Hotspur: Walker, Carr, Perry, Campbell, Edinburgh, Leonhardsen (Fox), Sherwood, Clemence, Ginola (Dominguez), Iversen, Armstrong

Arsenal: Seaman, Dixon, Keown, Adams, Winterburn, Ljungberg, Petit, Vieira, Overmars, Kanu, Bergkamp

Tottenham Hotspur v. West Ham United

Date: 11 March 2001

Location: Upton Park

Match title: FA Cup quarter-final

Attendance: 26,048

The 1999/00 season under manager George Graham had been disappointing but, as usual, the new campaign brought with it fresh optimism for Spurs fans. The back end of the previous season had seen Spurs purchase a whole host of promising youngsters in the highly rated attacking midfielders Simon Davies and Matthew Etherington from Peterborough United, the extremely tall centre-back Anthony Gardner from Port Vale and the versatile Gary Doherty from Luton Town. These players, coupled with the young, home-grown defenders who had already made the breakthrough at White Hart Lane (Luke Young and, most vitally, the future club captain Ledley King), gave fans reason to believe the future of the club was extremely bright. What Tottenham needed now was an influx of big-name stars to complement the younger generation and the established performers already in the side such as Campbell, Perry, Freund, Sherwood, Iversen and Ferdinand.

Ginola had just been sold to Aston Villa but Spurs fans were soon to have a new hero when Graham swooped to sign the diminutive Ukrainian striker Sergei Rebrov from Dynamo Kiev. One of the leading scorers in the history of the Champions League (former European Cup), Rebrov had been much coveted by both AC Milan and Arsenal, and the fact that he signed for Spurs – not even in European competition – was seen as a major coup for the club. Spurs had tracked Rebrov for a long time and, when he was signed for a club-record fee of £11 million, great excitement was felt at White Hart Lane. It was by far the biggest stir Spurs had caused in the transfer market since Klinsmann had arrived at the club for the first time. As well as Rebrov, Graham again raided recently relegated Wimbledon for the excellent Scottish goalkeeper Neil Sullivan and the tough-tackling left-back Ben Thatcher, a player tipped for England honours.

It all created a huge wave of optimism ahead of the season opener against one of the newly promoted sides, Ipswich Town at a sunny White Hart Lane. Rebrov enjoyed a wonderful debut, playing a huge part in two of the Spurs goals and almost bringing the house down with a beautiful strike from outside the area with the outside of his foot that hit the bar. Spurs won that game 3–1 but, alas, soon slipped back into the inconsistent form that had plagued their league campaigns of recent seasons. Rebrov played well but never hit the heights expected of him, while the season also featured the ongoing saga of Sol Campbell's contract situation. The inspirational centre-back and club captain was out of contract at the conclusion of the season and had long been stalling over the signing of a new contract at Spurs. Few thought he would actually desert Spurs, but the longer the situation dragged on, the more concerned Tottenham fans became. On the plus side, King was already showing maturity beyond his years in his first full season in the side. A natural defender, he was asked to play in the centre of midfield most of the time by Graham, a role he adapted to with the coolness and grace of a seasoned professional. Davies too impressed greatly when given his chance, showing he could be the speedy, goalscoring threat from midfield the club had been without since Ginola's departure.

With the league campaign seen as little more than a building block towards the future after Christmas, it was again the FA Cup that provided the magic for Spurs fans. Leyton Orient were beaten 1–0 in the third round and, after falling behind at Charlton in the next round, Spurs turned on the style to win 4–2. Stockport County were

Tottenham Hotspur 3	West Ham United 2
Rebrov (2),	Pearce,
Doherty	Todorov

Tottenham Hotspur v. West Ham United

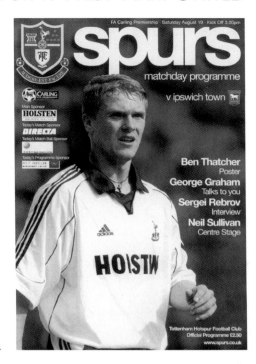

Spurs v. Ipswich Town, 2000.

thrashed 4–0 at White Hart Lane in the fifth round, with King and Davies (twice) getting on the scoresheet, and that win set up a quarter-final clash with London rivals West Ham at Upton Park. The game was to be one of the most exciting of the George Graham era. Apart from the wins at Leyton Orient and Charlton in the FA Cup, Spurs had been awful away from home all season, registering just one win at Manchester City. West Ham, under the seemingly anti-Tottenham manager Harry Redknapp, were a strong side full of quality players such as a young trio of midfielders tipped for future England stardom in Frank Lampard, Joe Cole and Michael Carrick, as well as the lanky but supremely skilled striker Fredi Kanoute and the inspirational yet hot-headed Italian forward Paolo Di Canio. Both Kanoute and Carrick would sign for Spurs in future years.

West Ham were slight favourites, but Spurs had the history and, on this day, they also had with them inspiration rarely seen throughout the season. Graham opted for an unusual 3-5-2 formation, with Young playing at left wing-back and Iversen, normally a target man of a centre forward, playing in the same role on the right. Sherwood – in fine form – was missing with injury, so squad player Stephen Clemence (son of former goalkeeper Roy) took his place in the middle with King and Freund as Spurs looked to diffuse the attacking threat of West Ham's young, talented midfield.

In a white-hot atmosphere with both sets of supporters singing their hearts out, it was a controlled Spurs that were by far the better team in the first half, the lively Rebrov shooting over and Ferdinand having a shot blocked

---

Tottenham Hotspur: Sullivan, Perry, Campbell, Doherty, Iversen, Freund, Clemence, King, Young, Rebrov, Ferdinand (Korsten)

West Ham United: Hislop, Winterburn, S. Pearce, Stimac, Dailly, Schemmel (Todorov), Lampard, Cole, Carrick, Di Canio, Kanoute

113

Tottenham Hotspur v. West Ham United

George Graham was the somewhat controversial selection to replace Christian Gross.

by the West Ham defender Stuart Pearce. Spurs were on top and, just after the half-hour mark, the deadlock was broken. A spell of pressure led to a throw-in down the left touchline. Freund hurled the ball into the West Ham area and as the ball cleared Iversen and a challenging defender, there was Rebrov waiting in behind. The Ukrainian swept in a left-foot volley into the top of the West Ham goal to give Spurs the lead. Spurs were well in command, but gave away a poor equaliser just before the break. Kanoute was adjudged to have been fouled some twenty-five yards out and, as he had so many times before in his great career, the veteran former England defender Stuart Pearce stepped up to take the free-kick. He proceeded to drill a bullet past Sullivan.

When Kanoute wasted a good chance early in the second half, Spurs stepped up a gear and grabbed hold of the game. On fifty-seven minutes, a long clearance by Sullivan was flicked on by the head of Ferdinand and scampering through to slide a cross-shot past Shaka Hislop in the West Ham goal was Rebrov; the little striker elated by his second goal of the game. Then, four minutes later, Spurs appeared to have the game won when Doherty headed home a Rebrov corner at the far post to put Spurs 3–1 ahead.

Spurs had worked extremely hard to keep West Ham at bay, with Young, Freund, King, Clemence and Iversen giving tremendous effort to dominate the midfield. The forwards had done their jobs, now it was the turn of the defence and goalkeeper Sullivan to try and thwart the home side as they poured forward to try and get back in the game. The Bulgarian substitute Todorov pulled one back on seventy-two minutes and there then followed an all-out assault on the Spurs goal. But Spurs had worked too hard to throw the game away at the death, and Sullivan made the save of the game to deny a late long-range effort from Cole.

As the final whistle went, the overjoyed Spurs players saluted the tremendous support their travelling fans had given them. It had been a total team performance, although the outstanding Sullivan and two-goal hero Rebrov stole most of the limelight.

Sadly, for George Graham and Spurs, this was to be the end of the joy. Five days later, with a new chairman in the form of ENIC's Daniel Levy (who took the place of Sugar) at the helm, Graham was sacked. Levy stated he wanted a true Tottenham man in charge, and the man he turned to was possibly the greatest player in the club's history, Glenn Hoddle. It was a controversial move as Hoddle had done well with Southampton (whose chairman Rupert Lowe made a huge public fuss about him leaving), and had previously had a successful but ultimately fruitless period in charge of England. His reign with the national side had come to an embarrassing end when, believing that his words were off the record, he made some ill-chosen comments that were relayed through the press by a journalist and, on the advice of none other than the Prime Minister, Hoddle was forced to leave his position. Whether this was justified can be argued strongly one way or the other. Nevertheless, Hoddle was given a hero's welcome on his return to Spurs.

Incredibly, Hoddle's first game in charge was the semi-final against Arsenal. Spurs took an early lead through Doherty, but when Campbell was injured the writing was on the wall, and Spurs succumbed 2–1 to a clearly superior side. The Hoddle era had begun.

TOTTENHAM HOTSPUR v. MANCHESTER UNITED

Date: 29 September 2001

Location: White Hart Lane

Match title: FA Premiership

Attendance: 36,038

The biggest news in the build-up to the start of Glenn Hoddle's first full season in charge of Spurs was the defection of captain and star centre-back Sol Campbell. His contract status had been a worry for Spurs fans for quite some time, with Manchester United reportedly having been prepared to pay £20 million for his services a couple of years previously, but when he did not re-sign during the 2000/01 season, it became obvious that Campbell would be leaving on a Bosman free transfer. It was bad enough that Spurs would not be receiving a penny for their prized asset, but the club Campbell chose to join was the real reason why Spurs fans now label their one-time idol as 'Judas'. When Campbell signed for Arsenal it was as if anything was now possible in the world of football and was a bitter indication that Spurs were no longer considered one of the major players in the Premiership. A big club? Yes. A historically significant club? Definitely. But a major player or force? No way; why else would an England centre half leave one of the biggest names in English football and the only club he had ever known – one he claimed was in his blood – and join that club's fiercest rivals?

Campbell's departure hit Spurs hard. Hoddle had always favoured playing three centre-backs with wing-backs on either side, and now the focus was shifted to ENIC to prove they could back up their talk of moving Spurs in the right direction by providing Hoddle with the funds to build his side. Hoddle opted for experience in that first season, bringing striker Teddy Sheringham back to the Lane from Manchester United on a free transfer before splashing some of ENIC's cash to sign elegant Yugoslav international defender Goran Bunjevcevic from Red Star Belgrade, left-footed Christian Ziege, the German international, from Liverpool, Uruguayan goal-scoring midfielder Gustavo Poyet from Chelsea and American goalkeeper Kasey Keller from Spanish club Rayo Vallecano to provide cover for Sullivan. But after an inconsistent start to the season in which both Bunjevcevic and Gary Doherty were lost to long-term injuries, Hoddle raided his former club Southampton to sign centre-back Dean Richards, infuriating Rupert Lowe in the process. The £8.1 million that it took to snare Richards seemed a huge amount for a player who had never been considered England quality, but he was greeted warmly by the Spurs fans. Richards could not have been thrown into a more scorching fire as Manchester United arrived at White Hart Lane for his debut, and the big defender was sure to be tested by the likes of David Beckham, Paul Scholes, Andy Cole, Juan Sebastian Veron and Ruud van Nistelrooy. What followed was one of the most remarkable games in Premiership history, and proved that football really can be a game of two halves.

The first half saw Spurs play the best football they would ever display under Hoddle as they literally dominated a fine United team. Spurs were first to every ball, passing superbly, attacking in waves and defending so well that United were restricted to long shots. After a quarter of an hour Richards announced himself royally to the Spurs crowd courtesy of a dream moment. As Ziege swept in a corner, there was the defender stooping low at the near post to head the ball past French goalkeeper Fabien Barthez. After twenty-five minutes, Spurs raced to a two-goal lead. Taricco won the ball and began a move that resulted in Poyet setting up Ferdinand to drill past Barthez. Spurs were on another level and, after going two goals ahead, their football began to flow. Even Freund – normally the most ungraceful player in the side – brought roars from the crowd as he successfully directed

---

Tottenham Hotspur 3

    Richards, Ferdinand,

    Ziege

Manchester United 5

    Cole, Blanc, van Nistelrooy,

    Veron, Beckham

a cheeky back-heeled pass. Inspired by the fans and in full flight, Spurs attacked again late in the first half. Freund sent a hopeful ball down the right flank but, as the United defence stalled, Poyet ran through to take control. Floating a delightful cross to the back post, the ball was met by Ziege – who had charged up from the back – and the German dived full length to cushion a beautiful header past Barthez for a 3–0 lead. As the whistle blew for half-time, every Spurs fan in the ground stood and applauded what had been a scintillating and wonderfully executed first-half performance. People could hardly believe what they had witnessed. But the sceptical maintained United could not be as powerfully bullied in the second half, and many agreed Spurs had to guard against surrendering an early goal to their visitors.

After just forty-five seconds of the second half, United had scored. Gary Neville crossed from the right and Cole thumped home a header from close range. All of a sudden the Spurs back three were being charged at as the United machine bore down on them like an angry rhinoceros. The veteran French sweeper Laurent Blanc headed home a Beckham corner on fifty-eight minutes,

Glenn Hoddle's return to the club as manager was a popular move with the fans.

and the comeback was on in earnest. United now looked as though they would score with every attack as Spurs shrank emphatically into their shell. Still Hoddle made no adjustments or substitutions and on seventy-seven minutes United were level. Silvestre cruised down the left and a simple van Nistelrooy header met his cross. Spurs players looked at each other in disbelief, the visiting fans erupted and their players smelled blood. Four minutes later, United led. The Argentine schemer Veron was allowed to waltz into the left side of the Spurs box and flash a shot beyond Sullivan and into the net for 4–3. Rebrov came on late but it made no difference, Spurs had gone out like a light. When Beckham was given the time to control Solskjaer's cross and pick his spot in the final moments, even the Tottenham players and supporters had accepted their fate.

It was a truly remarkable game and a fine comeback by United. But the lasting impression from the game was the fact that Tottenham had proved inept at holding onto a staggering advantage and had simply collapsed. True, United were an exceptional side, but no top-flight team should throw away a three-goal half-time lead, and for that, the first real rumblings of concern regarding Hoddle's tactical skills were unveiled. It had, nevertheless, been a game for the ages, and will long be remembered as one of the most incredible games ever witnessed at White Hart Lane.

Tottenham Hotspur: Sullivan, Perry, Richards, King, Taricco, Poyet, Anderton (Rebrov), Freund, Ziege, Sheringham, Ferdinand

Manchester United: Barthez, G. Neville, Johnsen, Blanc, Irwin (Silvestre), Veron, Beckham, Butt (Solskjaer), Scholes, van Nistelrooy, Cole

Tottenham Hotspur v. Chelsea

Date: 23 January 2002

Location: White Hart Lane

Match title: League Cup semi-final 2nd leg

Attendance: 36,100

If Tottenham Hotspur have had a bogey team in the modern era of the game, one team that has proved a constant thorn in their side, then that club is undoubtedly their London neighbours Chelsea. The last time Spurs had beaten Chelsea had come in the league back in 1990 when goals from David Howells and Gary Lineker gave them a 2–1 win at Stamford Bridge. The drought at White Hart Lane was even longer, with the last Spurs victory coming way back in 1987 courtesy of a sole strike from Belgian Nico Claesen. So after disposing of Torquay United, Tranmere Rovers, Fulham and Bolton in the preceding four rounds of the 2001/02 League Cup, it did not bode well for Tottenham and their supporters when it was Chelsea that the club were drawn to face in the two-legged semi-final. Chelsea had beaten Spurs 3–2 in the league at White Hart Lane earlier in the season (and would win 4–0 at Stamford Bridge later in the season, as well as 4–0 at White Hart Lane in the quarter-final of the FA Cup), and naturally started as hot favourites to claim a place in the final at Cardiff's Millennium Stadium. True to form, Chelsea took the first leg at Stamford Bridge, but only after Spurs had dominated the game for long periods, proving they were ready to rise to the challenge of the semi-final. Dutch striker Jimmy Floyd Hasselbaink scored two goals, one early in the first half and the other a fabulous free-kick thirteen minutes from time to give Chelsea a 2–1 lead going into the game at White Hart Lane. Spurs had played above expectations at Stamford Bridge, controlling the middle portion of the game, and were rewarded for their efforts when Les Ferdinand (who had earlier missed a golden chance) rounded goalkeeper Carlo Cudicini to give Spurs a valuable goal.

The atmosphere inside White Hart Lane on the Wednesday night in late January was nothing short of electric. Hoddle opted for his favoured 3-5-2 formation with Chris Perry, the rapidly emerging Ledley King and young Anthony Gardner – playing by far the biggest game of his career in the absence of the cup-tied Dean Richards – in defence, flanked by wing-backs Mauricio Taricco and Simon Davies. The German midfielder Steffen Freund had been enjoying a fine season, but his injury in the first leg had allowed Tim Sherwood, never the most popular player among the Spurs faithful, to come back into the side, where he had been most impressive at Stamford Bridge, rightly keeping his place alongside Anderton and Poyet in midfield. Ferdinand – so often missing during his Spurs career – was out again with injury, but captain Teddy Sheringham returned to the team having missed the first leg, and partnered Iversen up front. Chelsea, managed by the likeable Italian Claudio Ranieri, were a team fast on the rise, and fielded many of the stars from their fine squad, including strong English centre-back John Terry, excellent French defenders William Gallas and Marcel Desailly, blossoming central midfielder Frank Lampard, ex-Arsenal title-winner Emmanuel Petit and the top strike force of Hasselbaink and Iceland's Eidur Gudjohnsen, with the crafty Italian veteran Gianfranco Zola on the bench.

Any thoughts that Tottenham would play cautiously on the night were dispelled after only two minutes of what would be a pulsating match. A long ball from the right was dummied brilliantly by Sheringham and found its way to Taricco on the left. The Argentinian was allowed to make progress into the Chelsea box where he fired a shot at Cudicini. The Italian was able to block his effort, but Iversen reacted quickest to the loose ball and turned it into the net to give Spurs the lead. Level on aggregate and pumped full of adrenalin, Spurs were fired up.

Tottenham Hotspur 5

Iversen, Sherwood, Sheringham, Davies, Rebrov

Chelsea 1

Forsell

TOTTENHAM HOTSPUR v. CHELSEA

Every player wearing white rose to the occasion and gave his all, not allowing Chelsea the time or space to play. An aggressive tackle by Sheringham meant Chelsea's Dutch winger Boudewijn Zenden had to be carried off, and it got worse for the visitors on thirty-three minutes. A fierce Poyet effort was tipped over by Cudicini, giving Spurs a corner. In his first spell at Spurs, Sheringham had developed a classic corner-kick move where he would peel to the near-outer corner of the box where Anderton

The incident that led to Hasselbaink's sending off.

would drill it to him. The tactic worked on a regular basis, catching opponents unaware, but as Anderton sent a similar corner over against Chelsea, many wondered if there had been a miscommunication as Sheringham was nowhere in the vicinity. But the move had been perfectly crafted, as Sheringham in this instance was used as a decoy, and in his place Sherwood had the time to swivel and pick his spot with a cracking drive into the Chelsea net.

Spurs left the field at half-time to a standing ovation, even if some had the 5–3 loss to Manchester United from earlier in the season in the back of their minds. Chelsea were still very much in the game with the aggregate score 3–2 to Spurs but, five minutes into the second half, it was Spurs who pressed further ahead. Taricco fed Anderton down the left and his cross was cushioned back by the chest of Poyet and Sheringham was able to fire a shot of such power that Cudicini could only palm the ball into the net. Moments later and the gods really seemed to be smiling on Spurs. Chelsea had a corner but, as Sullivan came to gather the ball, the goalkeeper was impeded and a mini-melee broke out. Sheringham appeared to be struck in the face, and replays showed that Chelsea defender Mario Melchiot was the guilty party. Unbelievably, referee Mark Halsey sent off Hasselbaink, arguably Chelsea's most dangerous player and, despite much protesting, Chelsea were down to ten men. The Spurs fans were loving every moment of the match, and their joy turned into a carnival-like party when Davies struck to beat Cudicini to the goalkeeper's left on seventy-six minutes, and then the two substitutes combined to give Spurs a fifth goal on eighty-seven minutes – Leonhardsen crossing for Rebrov to finish easily.

The crowd were in full voice, and when Chelsea substitute Mikael Forsell grabbed a late consolation it barely interrupted the singing. At the final whistle, the smiles on the faces of Hoddle and the players were as wide as the White Hart Lane pitch. Tottenham's Chelsea hoodoo had been snapped in the most emphatic of ways, and they had presented their supporters with some long-awaited bragging rights. It was a night to remember at White Hart Lane, and Spurs had now reached their second League Cup final in three years.

Tottenham Hotspur: Sullivan, King, Perry, Gardner, Davies, Poyet (Leonhardsen), Sherwood, Anderton, Taricco, Sheringham, Iversen (Rebrov)

Chelsea: Cudicini, Gallas, Desailly, Terry, Melchiot (Zola), Petit (Forsell), Lampard, Zenden (Della Bonna), Stanic, Hasselbaink, Gudjohnsen

TOTTENHAM HOTSPUR v. BLACKBURN ROVERS

Date: 24 February 2002

Location: Millennium Stadium, Cardiff

Match title: League Cup final

Attendance: 72,500

The euphoria that came with the semi-final victory over Chelsea took a long time to die down at White Hart Lane. By the time the team arrived at Cardiff's impressive Millennium Stadium, it appeared to be a formality that the side would overcome the underdogs, the Graeme Souness-managed Blackburn Rovers. It was Hoddle's first final as manager of the club he loved, and it seemed destined that it would be he who would lead Spurs gloriously back into Europe.

Spurs were definite favourites on the day, although a number of Hoddle's selections raised eyebrows among the supporters. Both Anthony Gardner and Simon Davies – the pair magnificent in helping Spurs reach the final – were left on the bench. Their absence deprived Spurs of youth and pace – two traits that, as it transpired, would surely have been a benefit in this game – as Hoddle went with the likes of veterans Thatcher, Perry and Anderton, as well as the aging trio of Poyet, Sheringham and Ferdinand. Blackburn were largely unconsidered entering the match, mostly because of Tottenham's emphatic destruction of Chelsea a round earlier, yet with talented players like Damien Duff, David Dunn and Matt Jansen in their ranks, as well as a tough defence guarded by the outstanding American goalkeeper Brad Friedel, Rovers were always going to provide Spurs with a stern test.

With the game the first ever English cup final to take place under a closed roof, the game began surrounded by a wall of noise and a carnival of colour from both sets of fans following an emotional rendition of the national anthem. From the start, it was clear that Blackburn had a game plan. The midfield – led by the veteran Mark Hughes and the lively Dunn – were to disrupt the Tottenham central trio of Poyet, Anderton and Sherwood, while the electric Duff and the quick Keith Gillespie were given the green light to expose the Tottenham flanks. As it transpired throughout the game, the Spurs midfield was rarely able to seize control; dominated by a sharper, quicker, more determined Blackburn group. Even so, it was Spurs that carved out the more clear-cut early chances. A marvellous opportunity befell Ferdinand on nineteen minutes, as Poyet sent the striker clear down the left. Ferdinand was allowed a free run on the Blackburn goal and seemed sure to open the scoring. But he hesitated somewhat in shooting and, as he cut inside, Friedel was able to position himself to smother, pulling off a fine save in what would be a brilliant afternoon for the American. Spurs had other chances in the first half, with Ferdinand close with a header and the dangerous Ziege having a shot blocked but, as the half wore on, Blackburn steadily got into the flow of the game, with Duff in particular proving a menace down the Tottenham right flank. With Spurs hesitant in midfield, Gillespie picked up the ball that led to the opening goal. Running ominously into the Spurs box, Gillespie's shot was blocked by a Tottenham defender but Jansen was perfectly placed to shoot home the follow-up and give Rovers the lead. As the north end of the stadium erupted, the Tottenham supporters fell quiet in temporary shock. No team whose fans had sat in the south end of the stadium had ever won a final in Cardiff, and now Spurs were losing, and they very nearly went 2–0 down as Blackburn began to dominate. Duff was causing havoc and fired in a shot that beat Sullivan and, when the ball rebounded to Gillespie, the winger looked sure to score, but contrived to put the ball wide under pressure from Thatcher. On thirty-three minutes, Spurs sprang to life. Poyet again released Ferdinand, this time down the right, and just

---

Tottenham Hotspur 1

Ziege

Blackburn Rovers 2

Jansen,

Cole

Tottenham Hotspur v. Blackburn Rovers

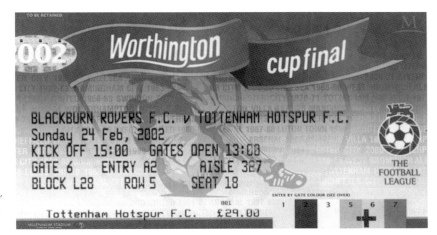

Spurs v. Blackburn Rovers, Worthington Cup final ticket, 2002

when it looked as though the striker had carried the ball too far, he was able to cut the ball back from the byline where – charging up from the back – Ziege met his pass with an accurate drive into the left side of the Blackburn net, finally beating the outstretched Friedel. 'Zie-ge, Zie-ge' cried out the Spurs fans, and the game was perfectly poised as half-time arrived, despite Ferdinand missing another great chance with a header just before the break. Spurs, although having made a few chances, had not passed the ball well or exuded the confidence of favourites, failing to impose themselves fully on the game, while it was Blackburn that had looked the more assured, and seemed ready to fight to the death.

Just before the hour mark, it was Spurs that had the chance that may have seriously altered the game. Bustling through the Blackburn defence, Poyet suddenly found himself with just Friedel to beat. Placing a high shot to the left side of the goal, Poyet looked on in disbelief as the ball cannoned back off the corner of bar and post. Following up the effort was Sheringham, but the Spurs captain – who was having a poor game by his standards – failed to connect sufficiently and the chance was gone. Ten minutes later disaster struck for Spurs. Ledley King, who had played with coolness and maturity, fluffed a header back to Sullivan and, instead of clearing his lines, he unfortunately directed a second header straight at Andy Cole, and the striker hit a weak shot that evaded Sullivan and crept in. It was a bitter blow but, to his credit, King was the one player who then drove Spurs on to try and find an equaliser, beginning numerous attacks from the back. Blackburn's defence was proving incredibly hard to breach and, with Davies on for Spurs to provide a spark, Tottenham found only two more opportunities to salvage the game. With two minutes remaining, King found Sheringham in the Rovers area, and as Sheringham went down, there were huge appeals for a penalty, but referee Graham Poll waved play on. Then, right at the death, Spurs looked sure to equalise when Sheringham found another substitute, Steffen Iversen, and the Norwegian gently cushioned a header back to Ferdinand. But it had not been Ferdinand's day, and he squandered another glorious chance as his header was well saved by Friedel. The Spurs fans were on their feet, they could not believe it, but seconds later the whistle blew and Tottenham had lost.

Tottenham Hotspur: Sullivan, King, Perry, Thatcher, Taricco (Davies), Poyet (Iversen), Sherwood, Anderton, Ziege, Sheringham, Ferdinand

Blackburn Rovers: Friedel, Bjornebye, Berg, Johansson, Taylor, Dunn, M. Hughes, Duff, Gillespie (Hignett), Jansen (Yordi), Cole

TOTTENHAM HOTSPUR *v.* BLACKBURN ROVERS

Spurs v. Blackburn, Worthington Cup final
programme, 2002

As the Blackburn players and supporters celebrated ecstatically, Spurs players slumped to the ground and their fans trudged away disappointed. One had to feel particularly sorry for King. It was indeed his error that had ultimately cost Spurs the match, yet here was a player who would develop into arguably Tottenham's finest home-grown player since Hoddle himself. King's confidence was visibly dented after the game, his play littered with silly mistakes for the remainder of the season. But the following season, he progressed again, and kept on progressing to the point where he starred as a member of England's Euro 2004 squad in Portugal and was eventually named Tottenham's club captain during the 2004/05 season. For Hoddle though, the chance of guiding the club into Europe in his first full season in charge had vanished, and sadly, for a man labelled as a saviour on his return to White Hart Lane, the remainder of his reign was frustratingly uneventful. After the Worthington Cup failure, Spurs saw their form dip, and they finished ninth in the Premiership. The following season was even more disappointing; a tenth-placed league finish accompanied by early exits in both cups. What was more worrying was that Spurs were not playing the sort of football one would expect with Hoddle as manager, too often content with long-ball football and frequently lacking a cutting edge. It was clear that some of the older players who Hoddle had initially brought in were in need of replacing. Sheringham and Poyet were declining rapidly; Ziege was suffering terrible luck with injuries and Richards' form collapsed completely. Although Irish striker Robbie Keane proved a success when he was brought in from Leeds United, some of Hoddle's more speculative signings, such as Slovenia's tricky wide player Milenko Acimovic and young Belgian Jonathan Blondel – although not without talent – failed to make an impact, while former Liverpool and England midfielder Jamie Redknapp was also signed, but an injury-riddled career had left him only half the player he was at his peak, and he was not the answer for a team desperately lacking in pace, craft and ideas.

The signs were bad for Hoddle when the team lost their last three league games of 2002/03, including the very last one at home to Blackburn 4–0 when afterwards only half of the dispirited squad initially trudged out for the traditional end-of-season lap of honour, which was not only insulting to the fans, but also indicative of a squad and manager divided.

Tottenham Hotspur v. Blackburn Rovers

Christian Ziege (left) is congratulated by Sheringham after scoring the equaliser.

The 2003/04 season started woefully for Spurs. They had signed the tall, skilful front player Fredi Kanoute from relegated West Ham and had made a huge stir when landing one of Europe's most promising youngsters, FC Porto forward Helder Postiga, for over £6 million, yet four defeats in the first six games – including inexplicable home maulings by Fulham and Southampton – left the club in disarray. It was to be Hoddle who paid the price and, even though the team were clearly not progressing under his guidance, it was a sad day when he was sacked. The remainder of the season was probably the most farcical in Spurs history. With no manager, it was left to the director of football, David Pleat, to take control of the side. Pleat had led a fine Spurs side in 1987, but he was now in a no-win situation. He knew he was not a contender for the permanent position, yet he was not at liberty to discuss who would be the new manager – a man chairman Daniel Levy claimed was already being consulted with over future transfers. The season was awash, Spurs lost a whopping 19 league games, Postiga failed to score a goal until January, and they even managed to get knocked out of the FA Cup 4–3 by ten-man Manchester City having led 3–0 at half-time. The one bright spot was the unexpected signing of young striker Jermain Defoe from West Ham in the January transfer window. Defoe proved sensational from the outset, scoring in a 4–3 win over Portsmouth on his debut. However, with an eventual league placing of fourteenth, all Spurs fans were relieved when the season came to a close, and all the attention now focused on who the new manager would be and in what direction Spurs were heading.

TOTTENHAM HOTSPUR v. MANCHESTER UNITED

Date: 4 January 2005   **Match title:** FA Premiership
Location: Old Trafford   **Attendance:** 67,962

All the mystery surrounding the appointment of the new Spurs manager finally ended in the summer of 2004 as England embarked on their European Championship campaign in Portugal. The club had already appointed highly respected Frank Arnesen, formerly of PSV Eindhoven, as the sporting director, a role that basically accounted for the transfer of players to and from the club. For the 'head coach' role as it had been termed, many candidates had been rumoured to be interested in the position, including the well-regarded Italian coach Giovanni Trappatoni and the Celtic boss Martin O'Neill. But in the end, the task of taking responsibility for Tottenham Hotspur as a football team fell to Frenchman Jacques Santini, who at the time was manager of the French national side. Although little was known of Santini in England he was a fairly recognisable name, being in charge of a nation considered one of the best in world football. His English was poor, but Santini came with a good reputation, although there was some concern among Spurs fans when France played without flair in the European Championships, bowing out to surprise champions Greece in the quarter-finals. As well as Santini, the barrel-chested Martin Jol was appointed as assistant coach. Jol too was highly thought of among those in the know, particularly in his native Holland where he had enjoyed great success managing smaller clubs, and he had almost become Sir Alex Ferguson's assistant at Manchester United the season before. However, Jol was seen as more of a head coach type, and many wondered how having Arnesen, Santini and Jol on the staff would work, particularly given the problems the club had undergone when David Pleat was director of football with Glenn Hoddle as manager.

Nevertheless, the summer before the 2004/05 season brought great optimism and excitement among the supporters, and Spurs began recruiting players at a rate of knots, as Arnesen displayed his breadth of knowledge of the European and worldwide scene by bringing a whole host of players to the club – whether Santini wanted them or not. With the soon-to-be England number one, Paul Robinson, already on board having been signed from Leeds United at the end of the previous season, Ledley King returning from the European Championships with great credit at centre-back, Jermain Defoe – signed in the 2004 January transfer window from West Ham – already a fan favourite up front, where he had good support from two Hoddle signings in Robbie Keane and Fredi Kanoute, and Simon Davies expected to improve again, Arnesen had a solid base upon which to build. He first addressed the central-midfield area, signing Fulham's all-action warrior Sean Davis and exchanging the disappointing Helder Postiga for Porto's cultured Pedro Mendes – fresh from Champions League (European Cup) glory. Left-back Erik Edman, a star of Sweden's exciting European Championship run, was brought in, as was the tough-tackling, unknown Frenchman Noe Pamarot, who played right-back. The vastly experienced Moroccan centre half Nourredine Naybet was captured from Deportivo La Coruna shortly before the season kicked-off and, not long into the campaign, the much-coveted Michael Carrick was plucked from West Ham to give the midfield a natural playmaker with fine passing ability. In addition, youngsters were signed in abundance from all corners of the globe, including the Swiss teenager Reto Ziegler who was not expected to feature in his first season, yet became a regular on the left side of midfield as he proved a most pleasant surprise. Some of the other signings

---

Tottenham Hotspur 0   Manchester United 0

TOTTENHAM HOTSPUR v. MANCHESTER UNITED

Pedro Mendes scored the famous 'goal' at Old Trafford.

featured too, such as full-back Timothee Atouba of Cameroon, while the likes of Calum Davenport (signed from Coventry City) and the Brazilian teenager Rodrigo Defendi were considered most promising defenders for the future.

The season started in solid fashion for Spurs as they went unbeaten in their first six games. However, only four goals were scored in that time (three by the blossoming Defoe) and already Tottenham were accused of becoming dull and boring under Santini, something that did not sit well with the fans. In their next five games, Spurs lost four times, scoring just two goals. Santini hardly spoke, the players seemed frustrated and there were rumours that all was not well within the club. Then, after the 2–0 defeat to Fulham at the end of October, the unthinkable happened as Santini resigned, citing personal problems. It emerged later that certain aspects of his job had upset the Frenchman, and once again it appeared that Spurs were in disarray, with a new manager (or head coach) having to be found.

Tottenham Hotspur: Robinson, Pamarot, Naybet, King, Edman, Marney, Pedro Mendes, Carrick, Ricketts (Gardner), Ziegler, Keane

Manchester United: Carroll, P. Neville, Heinze, Ferdinand, Silvestre, Ronaldo (Spector), Giggs (Bellion), Keane, Scholes, Fletcher, Smith

Tottenham Hotspur v. Manchester United

But waiting in the wings was Martin Jol; a far more colourful character, a man who spoke good English and one who seemed to have a far better grasp of man-management than Santini. Despite a bizarre 5–4 home defeat by Arsenal in one of his first games, Jol quickly balanced the Spurs side, combining strong defending with slicker attacking play. The team enjoyed a run of six wins in seven games before the New Year and, almost instantly, Jol had the supporters thinking optimistically again. The January transfer window again saw Spurs recruit heavily, signing the Nottingham Forest duo of Republic of Ireland winger Andy Reid and England Under-21 centre-back Michael Dawson in an £8 million deal, as well as the talented Egyptian striker Mido on an eighteen-month loan from Italian club Roma.

One of the most interesting games of the 2004/05 season came against Manchester United in January and illustrated the new-found resolve, character and spirit installed in the team by Jol. Spurs were missing the likes of Simon Davies, Sean Davis, Defoe and Kanoute for one reason or other, with the likes of young midfielders in Dean Marney, Rohan Ricketts and Ziegler all in the line-up. United had a strong side out, including England defender Rio Ferdinand, dynamic captain Roy Keane, in-form Welshman Ryan Giggs and striker Alan Smith.

The early stages saw United enjoy much of the pressure, with Smith forcing Robinson into a fine, full-length save after twelve minutes and, not long after, the same player floated over a dangerous cross that somehow missed everyone in the Spurs area. Smith again looked sure to open the scoring on thirty-six minutes when he found himself in space in the Spurs box, only for Robinson to block his shot heroically. Having withstood the early charge, Spurs began to look more accomplished as the game wore on, King dominating at the back, and both Carrick and Pedro Mendes displaying grace and vision in midfield, while Robbie Keane soldiered on bravely on his own up front as Spurs crammed the central areas, disrupting the home side's rhythm. The second half saw Tottenham begin to take control, with their main moment of danger arriving when Pamarot almost turned a United cross into his own net. Somehow, the ball hit the inside of a post and bounced to safety.

Tottenham had produced a performance of real character at Old Trafford under Jol, a performance that many of his predecessors would have struggled to achieve. Spurs had not won at Old Trafford in the league since 1989 and, in the dying moments, they were cruelly denied the chance to end that drought. The United goalkeeper Roy Carroll had advanced some way out of his goal to make a clearance and, as the ball bounced around the halfway line, it fell to Pedro Mendes. In one instinctive move, the Portuguese player swivelled and hit a high shot that looped towards the United goal. Back-pedalling, Carroll seemed to have the shot covered, but as he went to catch the ball, he spilled it into his own net before palming it away from a full yard behind the goal line. The Spurs fans went wild with excitement at the opposite end as they realised what had happened; yet astonishingly neither the linesman nor the referee, Mark Clattenburg, awarded the goal. Replays proved the ball had blatantly crossed the line, and Spurs had been robbed of a famous victory.

It would have been much worse if Robinson had not dived superbly to claw away a last-gasp free-kick from Argentinian full-back Gabriel Heinze, but at the final whistle, Spurs had extended their unbeaten streak to eight games, and earned themselves much respect in the process. Naturally, the question of television replays being introduced during games to decide important moments was thrown forward in the wake of the 'Mendes goal', for it truly was a terrible decision, and had denied Spurs what would have been a terrific result.

Tottenham proved resilient for the remainder of the season, enjoying deep runs in both cup competitions and achieving a high league position. With Arnesen again working overtime to improve the playing staff, strong Finnish midfielder Teemu Tainio and experienced Canadian full-back Paul Stalteri were signed from Auxerre and Werder Bremen respectively, while promising English youngsters Tom Huddlestone, Wayne Routledge and Aaron Lennon arrived from Derby County, Crystal Palace and Leeds United. But just as Spurs were settling in to

Jermain Defoe, one of the brightest young hopes at White Hart Lane.

the blossoming format of the Arnesen/Jol partnership, Premiership winners Chelsea approached the former. After Spurs rightfully received considerable compensation, Arnesen left for Stamford Bridge.

Yet there is a feeling that, regardless of Arnesen, Spurs are on the correct path at last. With the much-liked Dutchman in charge, a core of key players such as Robinson, King, Carrick, Dawson, Reid, Defoe, Keane and Mido entering their peak years, complemented by the recent signing of Dutch international midfielder Edgar Davids and a batch of very promising youngsters waiting in the wings, the future at Tottenham Hotspur is extremely bright, as the current squad look to emulate many of the great sides of the past in bringing the glory days and nights back to White Hart Lane.

Other sport titles published by Tempus

Tottenham Hotspur Football Club 1882-1952
ROY BRAZIER

Named after Harry Hotspur, Tottenham have always attracted the more style-conscious supporter. This book celebrates the first seven decades in the history of Tottenham Hotspur FC with over 200 images. The selection includes action shots, programmes, cartoons, team groups and other items of significant memorabilia that evoke the rich football heritage of the famous north London outfit.

0 7524 2044 5

Tottenham Hotspur Football Club Since 1953
ROY BRAZIER

Over the last fifty years London's most famous football club has enjoyed its fair share of highs and lows. Twice winning the First Division Championship and achieving six FA Cups, Tottenham have also enjoyed massive success in Europe during this time. This pictorial history also looks at the great names who have worn Tottenham shirts and will appeal to anyone with an interest in Tottenham Hotspur FC.

0 7524 2924 8

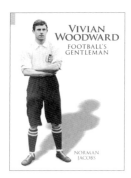

Vivian Woodward   Football's Gentleman
NORMAN JACOBS

Vivian Woodward led England to victory in both the 1908 and 1912 Olympic Games. An amateur throughout his career, he was famous for his sportsmanship and as an embodiment of the Corinthian spirit. Having signed for Tottenham Hotspur in 1902 he scored Spurs' first goal in League football and went on to become the best-known name in football. Woodward's biography will be a delightful read for any Spurs fan.

0 7524 3430 6

Forever England   A History of the National Side
MARK SHAOUL & TONY WILLIAMSON

From the days of amateur gentlemen of the 1870s to the present day, *Forever England* is an insightful and fascinating account of the history of the country's national football team. This enthralling narrative includes England team line-ups for key games, match reports and every group table involving England from all major tournaments, and is richly illustrated with over 200 images.

0 7524 2939 6

If you are interested in purchasing other books published by Tempus, or in case you have difficulty finding any Tempus books in your local bookshop, you can also place orders directly through our website

www.tempus-publishing.com